Creative
Stewardship

Creative Leadership Series

Creative
Stewardship

Richard B. Cunningham

Creative Leadership Series
Lyle E. Schaller, Editor

Abingdon Press/Nashville

CREATIVE STEWARDSHIP

Copyright © 1979 by Abingdon

Sixth Printing 1984

Library of Congress Cataloging in Publication Data

CUNNINGHAM, RICHARD B
  Creative stewardship.
  (Creative leadership series)
  1. Stewardship, Christian. 2. Christian giving. 3. Church finance.
  I. Title. II. Series.
  BV772.C779   248'.6   79-973

ISBN 0-687-09844-0

Scripture quotations are from the Revised Standard Version of the Bible,
copyrighted 1946, 1952, © 1971, 1973 by the Division of Christian Education
of the National Council of the Churches of Christ in the U.S.A., and are used
by permission.

MANUFACTURED BY THE PARTHENON PRESS AT
NASHVILLE, TENNESSEE, UNITED STATES OF AMERICA

To
Rebecca

Foreword

Creativity and *stewardship* are two words that are inextricably linked in any discussion of leadership in the churches. The good leader recognizes, as Richard Cunningham points out in the last chapter of this volume, that "human beings are the most valuable resource within the church." The creative leader understands that good stewardship includes helping people discover and develop their own unique gifts. The church is a place that nurtures these gifts.

The six volumes published thus far in this series represent an attempt to help leaders in the churches to be creative and to be good stewards of that which God has entrusted to us. In the first volume of this series Robert Kemper presents a variety of ways for the pastor and lay leaders to be good stewards of the opportunities that come with the beginning of a new pastorate. In the second volume, I have suggested how churches can reach and assimilate new members. The evangelistic imperative calls the churches to reach people with the good news that Jesus Christ is Lord and Savior. The stewardship responsibility requires the churches to be more intentional and effective in assimilating new members into that nurturing and caring fellowship of believers.

In the third and fourth volumes of this series Douglas Johnson and Speed Leas carry over the stewardship to the care of volunteers and the management of time. In several respects Doug Johnson's ideas parallel the last chapter of this volume. An effective network of volunteers requires good stewardship of the time, energy, talents, and gifts of members. Speed Leas discusses that finite resource, time, and presents several methods to enable each of us to be better stewards of that scarce commodity.

Peter Wagner uses a series of medical analogies in identifying specific diseases to which churches are vulnerable. In that volume in the series he explains how leaders can be good stewards by using several diagnostic techniques to identify, and sometimes to avoid, the maladies that may inhibit the faithful and obedient response of the churches to the call of the Lord.

In this volume Dick Cunningham offers to the leaders of the churches, both lay and clergy, the guidelines that will help them apply the principles and patterns of Christian stewardship as a model for creative living.

LYLE E. SCHALLER
Yokefellow Institute
Richmond, Indiana

Preface

What is in a word? Sometimes more than one knows!
Stewardship is a word I have heard since childhood, one I have
valued and tried to take seriously. But it broke open with new
meaning and more universal dimensions in 1971 as I
prepared a biblical study for a National Stewardship Seminar
at Glorieta, New Mexico, for denominational leaders,
sponsored by the Stewardship Commission of the Southern
Baptist Convention. With concentrated study, I discovered
what I instinctively knew. The word is packed with meaning
and potential creative application to all of life! The genesis of
this book took shape then and in many other conferences and
in writing that I have done on stewardship since that time. I
remain grateful that the practical leaders of stewardship
within my own communion desire a biblical-theological
foundation for their work.

This particular book evolves from the conviction that
theology and practice ought to go together. I have attempted
to translate major theological insights about stewardship into
comprehensible terms for people who are not theological
specialists. Theological readers will likely detect the theological streams that flow into the ideas, although because of the
brevity of the book I have not extensively noted references.
The book cites biblical passages for most of the major ideas.
These help to provide a systematic biblical understanding of
different aspects of stewardship. That is important because
the Bible is the frame of reference for many of the church's
stewardship practices. The biblical references offer preach-
ing-teaching starters for church leaders.

Our study begins with biblical-theological reflection and moves on to practical concerns of stewardship. Chapters 2 and 3 deal theologically with God, man, and the world. For readers with little theological training these chapters might demand just a bit of mind-stretching. For that reason, I have kept them in a more familiar biblical frame of reference. But the theological insights can greatly enrich one's understanding of more practical areas of stewardship. From there we will look at the steward's total responsibility in the world, the stewardship of material resources and of giving, and in the last chapter at the corporate stewardship of the church. Perhaps patterns and applications will emerge that will help Christian stewardship to become a model for creative living.

Contents

Creative
Stewardship

I
Exploration into Stewardship

The scene is a typical, average-sized American city. As a family drives past their church, they notice the bulletin board. It announces "Christian Stewardship" as the title of next Sunday morning's sermon. "Oh," sighs the husband, "it looks like the pastor is going to preach on money again!" That incident is more the rule than the exception. When many American Christians hear the word *stewardship*, its sound immediately unleashes a flood of thoughts about budgets, tithing, financial campaigns, pledge cards, offering envelopes, and catchy slogans. It also triggers conflicting emotions.

Such reactions are predictable, given the frequent American tendency to use the word mainly in the context of financial needs and fund-raising. No wonder for many people the word reverberates with the sounds of cash registers, promotion, programming, and selective economic application. The irony is that *stewardship* is a common word in the vocabulary of American churches, but a word subject to superficial definition, trivialization, and misunderstanding. The damaging result of limiting stewardship primarily to financial concerns is that the real nature of Christian giving cannot be understood in isolation from the wider horizons of stewardship. Consequently, many people never come to see the far-reaching implications of stewardship for how they live all of life.

For people who have heard only limited definitions of the term, it may be a shock to hear the claim that stewardship is among the most profound and comprehensive words in the

Christian vocabulary, when defined biblically and theologically. In fact, its meaning is no less than cosmic in scope, and it encompasses the whole of life. Stewardship is man's responsibility before God to live all of life within God's world according to the will of God as revealed in Jesus Christ.

Stewardship cannot be confined to any limited sphere of life. Stewardship responsibilities fall upon each individual and upon the whole human family in every conceivable social group and structure. The individual's stewardship responsibilities overarch his private life to include his involvement in the church and in all levels of society. Christian stewardship calls us to become creative partners with God, working together with him in his world, creating and achieving and serving his purposes. It opens the possibility at many levels of leaving the world a better place than we found it and moving it further toward God's goal for the whole creative process.

A Creative Model for Living

Stewardship, when properly conceived, provides a unique model for creative living. It is a key that can help to interpret and integrate various dimensions of the individual's life and the church's life and ministry. Conceptual models are vitally important, whether in a scientist's laboratory or in the laboratory of life. By the use of a model we sort out, arrange, simplify, clarify, and let an intelligible pattern emerge from among many individual facts or aspects of life. On the basis of the conceptual model, we can then interpret our experience as a basis for exploration or investigation into new and diverse areas of concern. A useful model for living must focus profound, multifaceted truth in simple and manageable principles. It must integrate various dimensions of life into a meaningful whole so that different aspects of life converge in a basic purpose or goal and are understood and lived in light of that goal.

The stewardship model has the possibility of doing that for

our understanding and living of life itself, much like Einstein's theory of relativity does it for our understanding of space-time in the universe. How do we develop a stewardship model for creative living? Perhaps the process should develop much like an artist paints a canvas. First, we will sketch the guidelines by going to the root meaning of the biblical words that are translated "steward" and "stewardship" and then to the classic parables of Jesus that specifically use the words. But the texture, depth, and color of the finished model require extensive filling in through explorations into the larger theological dimensions of stewardship.

Sketching a Stewardship Model

The original meaning of the Greek word translated into the English term "steward" is rooted in the idea of house manager. A similar idea is found in the major Hebrew term *ashur-beth,* which is translated "steward." It means literally "one who is over a house." The New Testament Greek word translated "stewardship" is *oikonomia.* It is a combination of two words: *oikos,* meaning "house," and *nemein,* meaning "to divide, distribute, or apportion." *Oikonomia* has various meanings in classical Greek, but its most direct reference is to the administration or management of a household—for example, in matters of food and drink. The *oikonomos,* which is translated "steward," was entrusted with the responsibility of managing the business affairs of a household. The word often referred to a slave who was given responsibility over money, property, goods, or other slaves. So the word carries the idea of a trustee, one to whom something of value is entrusted.[1]

The actual usage of these particular terms is limited in the New Testament. *Oikonomos* ("steward") is used only twenty times. *Epitropos,* a word also referring to a trustee, is used three times. *Oikonomia* ("stewardship") is used only seven times. However, both terms belong to a larger family of Greek words that taken together provide important insights into the nature of stewardship. But even more, substantial stewardship teachings occur in both the Old and New Testaments apart from the actual usage of stewardship words.

The stewardship theme, for example, is integral to the teachings of Jesus, although he only uses the terms *oikonomia* ("stewardship") and *oikonomos* ("steward") in the two parables of the wise and foolish servants (see Luke 12:42-48) and of the unrighteous steward (see Luke 16:1-18). However, a similar theme runs through numerous other parables such as Dives and Lazarus (see Luke 16:19-31), the rich fool (see Luke 12:16-21), the servants who kill the master's son (see Mark 12:1-12; Matt. 21:33-46; Luke 20:9-19), the unprofitable servant (see Luke 17:7-10), the unmerciful servant (see Matt. 20:1-16), the obedient and disobedient sons (see Matt. 21:28-32), the talents (see Matt. 25:14-30), and the pounds (see Luke 19:11-28).

The two parables in which Jesus uses specific stewardship vocabulary—the wise and foolish servants (see Luke 12:42-48) and the unrighteous steward (see Luke 16:1-18)—highlight the basic elements, motifs, and rationale of a model of Christian stewardship. Both parables, like most other parables of Jesus, are teachings about the Kingdom. They emphasize man's final accountability for his response to the coming Kingdom. But that accountability makes sense only in relation to other important elements of the parables.

The stewardship drama in the parables involves the three critical elements: master, servant, and estate. And there are the stewardship motifs of faithfulness to the master, wisdom, and the servant's accountability to the master for his actions. These motifs might better be understood today as freedom, responsibility, and accountability in our lives before God. The common themes are quite clear, whatever the differences in the parables. The master entrusts oversight and management of his estate to his steward during his absence, while retaining ownership of his property. The steward is the designated representative of the master and is responsible for managing all the owner's resources until he returns. He oversees the estate in genuine freedom without any detailed instructions. But he is expected to be faithful to the master, to act wisely, and, in unexpected situations, to make an independent creative response. The critical point of the parables is that the steward is ultimately accountable to the master for his exercise of stewardship trust.

An Economic Interpretation of the Stewardship Model

A stewardship model composed of these themes can be interpreted and applied in various ways. An economic interpretation is an example of a widespread superficial and limited approach to Christian stewardship. God is pictured as a kind of cosmic banker who lends man the material and financial resources of life. As a steward, man is charged to invest wisely and give back part of his earnings to God. He will finally be accountable to God for his faithfulness in returning to God the part of his wealth that is legitimately God's. Who has not heard the popular illustration "If you have ten apples, one of the apples is God's"? The implication of such an interpretation is clear and simple: Stewardship primarily concerns the material aspect of life!

The economic model of Christian stewardship is often developed in the context of church financial concerns, budgeting, and programming. Much modern stewardship development has been tied to a worthy desire to secure financial support for important institutional needs and ministries of the church. A frequent popular result is that Christian leaders are selectively drawn to biblical texts that appear to support established programs and are capable of being turned into slogans for raising money for vital commitments of the church.

Numerous dangers lurk in the economic interpretation of stewardship. For one thing, it represents carelessness in biblical interpretation. That often includes the selective and indiscriminate use of scriptural proof texts for prevailing practices, reading into passages what is not necessarily there, and ignoring the preparatory character of the Old Testament

19

revelation in relation to the New Testament. Another danger is the temptation to financial legalism that crushes personal responsibility and freedom and subordinates the value of Christian individuals to that of the churchly institution. One result of any institutional manipulation of individuals is the alienation of many person-centered Christians who are negated by such procedures. These people are then tempted to neglect not only the financial dimension of stewardship but also its potential as a model for creative living.

There are many deficiencies in the economic interpretation of the stewardship model. And yet there must be no mistake about one thing: The material aspect of life *is* a critical and *major* sphere of Christian stewardship. The question is whether the material or financial concern should be made the exclusive or, for that matter, even the dominant focus of Christian stewardship. To do so is to interpret man as an economic animal. A Marxist could easily agree with such an economic preoccupation and definition. Such a restricted definition ignores the meaning and actual usage of the biblical words and basic motifs for stewardship. The fact is that few passages using the specific stewardship words refer to money or giving.[2]

The economic interpretation fractures the wholistic biblical and theological understanding of man and his place in the purposes of God. One cannot separate possessions from the possessor nor can we separate what we do with what we have from what kind of persons we are. What we do with our material resources is simply one reflection among many of where our values lie and what kind of persons we are. God is concerned about our use of things and possessions primarily because he cares about us as persons. Personal life is central to the divine purpose in the universe, and our character is mirrored in many dimensions of life.

A Theological Interpretation of the Stewardship Model

There is another way of interpreting Christian stewardship so that it becomes a model for creative living.[3] When informed by a deeper biblical and theological insight, the stewardship model throws light on how life can be lived in all its dimensions. In the theological interpretation, the master is the creator-redeemer God. The steward is man, the intelligent creature made in God's image and redeemed into a personal relationship with him. The estate over which man exercises trusteeship is the world, the stage for the drama of creation and redemption. Stewardship then becomes multi-dimensional, even cosmic in scope, leaving no sphere of life untouched. In this view, stewardship cannot be understood or responsibly lived apart from setting the role of the steward within the purposes of God in creation and redemption.

A brief theological rationale can be stated for stewardship as a model for creative living. As creator and redeemer of the world, God is owner of all the world's resources. Out of grace and love, God makes man his free representative in exercising dominion over the created world. Thus the world is central to God's plan of granting life to intelligent beings made in his own image who can enter freely into personal relationships with God. Man is to honor and glorify God by using the gift of life and the world's resources in responsible freedom and faithful obedience to God's plan as revealed in Christ and for the benefit of the whole human family. The achievement of the divine purpose has been made possible by God's reconciliation of the world to himself through Jesus Christ, an incomparable gift that places an absolute demand upon the Christian believer. God holds man accountable for how he exercises this trust.

This comprehensive theological view of stewardship does not remain in ethereal clouds of theological splendor. It enters into and addresses in principle the concrete, practical issues of life as they affect the individual, the church, and society as a whole. Stewardship can actually become a model for creative living. It involves the individual's stewardship of his private life, including his physical, mental, and spiritual health; the use of his time, abilities, and material possessions;

his vocation and calling as a Christian; and his involvement in varied spheres of social life.

Stewardship principles also apply throughout life and the social network—to family, church, citizenship, business, industry, education, government, the arts, and social services. Stewardship particularly informs the life of the church and calls it to responsibility for management of its spiritual, material, and human resources in effective Christian community, ministry, and mission. In every sphere of human responsibility, the theological stewardship model for creative living can apply its basic principles and motifs to the practical flow of life. And in every situation the motifs of man's freedom, responsibility, and accountability become critical as they are understood within the purposes of God.

The theological interpretation of the stewardship model preserves the church's legitimate concern for economics, finances, and the institutional needs of the church. It stresses the importance of generous Christian giving but sets that emphasis in a far larger frame of reference and informs giving with profound theological insight. It cannot state ten simple steps to responsible Christian stewardship, because it draws upon the whole theology of creation and redemption. Consequently, it cannot satisfy people who want easy answers and specific rules for living. But it does invite people to venture forth into creative living.

The theological interpretation relates God, man, and the world and sets the role of man within the purposes of God. It integrates the multiple dimensions of life into a focused purpose but leaves open the implementation of that purpose to human freedom and creativity in a faithful response to the will of God. It brings together separate and contrasting spheres of life into an integrated universal model for living. The Christian, as an individual and as a member of the church and of the human family, is responsible for the gifts of creation and redemption in serving God's purposes for the cosmic process.

The Stewardship of Man
Within the Stewardship of God

The starting point for Christian stewardship, as for all distinctive Christian thought and practice, is the encounter with God through faith in Jesus Christ. Stewardship principles then grow out of reflection upon the mystery of human existence in light of that encounter. There we discover clues to the origin, meaning, purpose, and goal of life in relation to the radical claim upon our lives by the God who has graciously redeemed us in Jesus Christ, the lord of our lives. The encounter between God and man in Jesus Christ unites the divine initiative with the human response, grace with faith, and the divine gift with the divine demand.

The Stewardship of God

The stewardship of man can be comprehended only in relation to the stewardship of God. That is a strange assertion to people who have only thought of stewardship in human or financial terms. Actually, *stewardship* is one of the terms the New Testament uses to describe the divine purpose in creation and redemption. *Oikonomia* ("stewardship") is used of God in several theologically formative passages where it is usually translated "plan" or "dispensation." But it literally means "stewardship." When the term *stewardship* is related to God, it refers to the divine plan for history that is centered in Jesus Christ.[4]

Paul first speaks of the stewardship of God in I Corinthians and then makes it a central theme in Ephesians and Colossians. The classic passage and the most important unifying statement on the stewardship of God as a framework for understanding the stewardship of man is in Ephesians 1:3-14. Here the writer asserts that election in Jesus Christ is the purpose of creation. Believers, who are chosen in Christ before the foundation of the world, have been redeemed, destined, and appointed to live for the praise of

23

his glory. God has disclosed his purpose in Christ as "a plan [*oikonomian*] for the fulness of time, to unite all things in him, things in heaven and things on earth" (see Eph. 1:9-10). And the uniting of all things in Christ is for the church, which is his Body. God's purpose embraces the universe.

Jesus Christ is the link between divine stewardship and human stewardship. And that is at two levels. Jesus Christ is the redemption and revelation of God himself. In Paul's words, "in Christ God was reconciling the world to himself" (II Cor. 5:19). That redemption places a total claim upon the Christian and all the resources of his life. "You are not your own," says Paul, "you were bought with a price" (I Cor. 6:19-20). But the historic redeemer is also the agent of creation. In fact, Christ is the origin, meaning, and goal of the creative process. Colossians states that all things were created in him, through him, and for him, "that in everything he might be pre-eminent" (see Col. 1:15-18). The God whom the Christian encounters in Jesus Christ is the sovereign lord of life, both by right of creation and by right of redemption. In the encounter with God the Christian receives everything as a gift, and God demands everything the Christian is and has in the obedience that is faith (see Rom. 1:5).

Jesus Christ is also the most perfect and final revelation of the nature and purpose of God, the meaning of human life, and the values by which human beings are to live. Therefore, any informing of the meaning of Christian stewardship must center upon the revelation in Christ. John interprets Jesus as "the way, and the truth, and the life" (John 14:6). The New Testament witnesses to the divine purpose as revealed in Christ and establishes the criteria by which the steward ultimately will be held accountable for how he lives life. It clarifies that the future judge will be the resurrected, exalted Christ who is the reigning lord of history (see Phil. 2:9-11). The eternal purpose of God—and the meaning of Christian stewardship—are bound up with his redemption and revelation in Jesus Christ.

Stewardship Within the Family of God

God is owner, and man the steward. But God is also Father, and the steward his child. Christian stewardship is set within a family relationship into which the children of God have been redeemed by God through Christ. Our election in Christ alters the stewardship model. In the words of Ephesians, "He destined us in love to be his sons through Jesus Christ, according to the purpose of his will, to the praise of his glorious grace which he freely bestowed on us in the Beloved" (1:5-6). Paul underscores the difference: "So through God you are no longer a slave but a son, and if a son then an heir" (Gal. 4:7). God expects faithfulness from his own child.

Christian stewardship is a family affair. Jesus spoke often of God as his Father (see Mark 1:25, et al.) and instructs his disciples to address God as our Father (see Matt. 6:9). Jesus says that those who do the will of God are his brothers, sisters, and mother (see Mark 3:31-33). And those who suffer for his sake will receive a hundredfold repayment within God's family household (see Mark 10:29 f.). God's family is centered in the church (see Eph. 2:19).

The parable of the prodigal son provides a classic illustration of stewardship within the family structure (see Luke 15:11-24). Here the relationship between father and sons is more important than the issue of possessions. Out of love the father allowed freedom for his sons, even when the misuse of freedom led to disobedience and disaster. When the prodigal son returned from his wanderings to his father's house he requested that he be allowed to be only a servant in his father's house. But then came the surprise. When the boy again became obedient to his father, the father received him back as a son, with full family rights to the wealth of the household. Paul makes a similar point when he says, "For all who are led by the Spirit of God are . . . children of God, and if children, then heirs, heirs of God and fellow heirs with Christ" (Rom. 8:14-17).

Americans who have experienced the breakdown of authority within the family must be careful to grasp what this father-child relationship means. The Bible's picture of the steward's exercising trust over a household reflects a patriarchal family relationship where there is shared ownership and responsibility. Members of the family have rights only as they respect the rights and authority of the father. The spiritual parallel is the sovereignty of our heavenly Father who loves his children with an incomparable love. But he expects them to live responsibly in faithfulness to his will as they exercise their individual freedom within the household. The steward's freedom must be used responsibly, in obedience to God's will, given out of gratitude for God's goodness.

Dimensions of Man's Stewardship

Man's stewardship touches every aspect of life. It involves the life of each individual, the church, and every grouping in society. Each individual is accountable for how he manages every part of his personal life. The Christian steward realizes that he has only one life to live and must therefore live it well. All of his individual life's resources—the gifts of creation and redemption—are a trust from God and are to be used to fulfill God's purposes. Those gifts include our limited time, our personhood and relationships, our abilities, and our spiritual and material resources—every facet of life.

Christian stewardship also involves profound social dimensions. The divine-human encounter not only reconciles the individual to God but also relates the individual Christian to the whole of society in a new way—to the redeemed within the church and alongside unbelievers outside the church. To be in Christ is to be a member of the Christian community. To be a child of God is to be sister and brother within the family of faith. Christians live together within the church with common interests and mutual purposes, committed to a servant ministry and mission to the world.

The church is a community of stewardship where each Christian surrenders some of his independence and autonomy without abandoning personal responsibility. The Christian steward discovers his gifts and responsibilities within Christ's church and participates responsibly in the church's life, ministry, and mission. It is a total participation that involves personhood, time, abilities, and all spiritual and material resources. To be in Christ is to become a fellow worker alongside other workers with God in and through the church (see Phil. 1:5). As a member of the church, the individual steward shares in the corporate stewardship of the church as the church fulfills its role and manages its resources in serving the purposes of God in the world.

Christian stewardship also involves life in the world. The divine-human encounter calls for the Christian to live distinctively as a Christian within the structures of the world that God has reconciled to himself in Christ. There he is to be the Christian presence and witness as he labors with all human beings within the orders of creation to serve the needs of the human family. Jesus' formula is to be in but not of the world (see John 17:16-17). Christian stewardship requires the steward to meet his basic human obligations in society, work, government, culture, marriage, and family life, even in the care of the ecological system of our planet and the universe. The Christian steward works with all people for human rights, justice, equality, peace, equitable distribution of the world's resources, and the care of the good earth. As a steward in the world, the Christian labors with God to bend the secular historical process toward the horizons of the coming kingdom of God.

Because Christian stewardship is so universal in scope, it cannot be fully understood apart from being interpreted by a theology of creation and redemption. Theology and the practical concerns of life should always be related. However, to combine a full theology of creation and redemption with a detailed treatment of such all-embracing practical stewardship concerns is obviously too ambitious for a small book. So

27

the book will treat selective theological principles concerning God, man, and the world that are basic to an informed understanding and practice of Christian stewardship. Such principles should then be capable of informing all areas of the practice of stewardship, from those of the individual through every level and grouping of society.

Chapters 2 and 3 will develop a series of serious theological principles that focus critical insights about the nature of God's ownership of the world, man's stewardship, and the nature of the world over which man is steward. The author hopes that they will be intelligible to readers who are not theological experts without oversimplifying complex theological problems. These strictly theological chapters will then be applied in the remainder of the book—using biblical, theological, and practical ideas—to important concerns in living out our Christian stewardship. Along the way we will provide useful preaching and teaching resources for church leaders. Because of the church's interest in financial stewardship, chapters 5, 6, and 7 will treat the stewardship of material resources and giving.

II
The Divine-Human Drama

Life is the drama of creation and redemption. "Christian Stewardship" is the title. God and man are the chief actors, and the world is the stage. God is author, director, and lead actor of the drama. He also owns the theater and will drop the final curtain. And yet he allows man as actor to make his own innovative contributions to the script, so that Christian stewardship becomes a creative collaboration of God and man, a divine-human venture into God's future.

All the drama's action revolves around the important elements, that God is owner of the world, man the steward, and the world the estate for which man is responsible. The drama's plot hinges on the purpose of God, the nature and role of man, the nature and purpose of the world, and the meaning of life and how it is to be lived. The pivotal event on which the story turns is God's mighty act of redemption and revelation in Jesus Christ.

The stewardship drama can be understood only within the context of the doctrines of creation and redemption. Human stewardship must be defined only in relation to God's stewardship—God's plan and purpose in creation and redemption. In this chapter we will reflect theologically upon the stewardship roles of God and man in light of selected relevant principles from the doctrines of creation and redemption. We will highlight those critical insights as formal theological principles about the nature of God's ownership of the world and man's stewardship that should inform every aspect of the practice of Christian stewardship.

God the Owner

Christian stewardship asserts that, as creator and as redeemer, God is owner of the world and the master of man. Those are strange and antiquated words to some contemporary ears. Like ancient Prometheus, many modern people sometimes get an inflated estimate of their own power and greatness. Algernon Charles Swinburne has stated the anthem of many moderns: "Glory to Man in the highest! for man is the master of things."

Master of all things? Man is often not even master of himself. And many of life's most critical elements are beyond our control, such as our birth or genetic heritage or death. But when measured against the immensity of a universe containing more stars than there are grains of sand on all the beaches of our planet, our individual lives shrink into cosmic insignificance. As the ancient psalmist expressed it, "When I look at thy heavens, the work of thy fingers, / the moon and the stars which thou hast established; / what is man that thou art mindful of him?" (Ps. 8:3-4).

But the psalmist's question is, "What is man that *thou* art mindful of him?" A theology of creation and redemption defines the nature of the universe and the significance and meaning of man in relation to God. In biblical thought, the universe is not self-explanatory. Rather it is the creative work of God, a cosmic panorama superbly crafted by the finger of God himself that draws man's eyes to the greatness of the Creator. The mind sensitive to that creative power and presence can only respond with, "O Lord, our Lord, / how majestic is thy name in all the earth!" (Ps. 8:9).

The vastness and grandeur of the universe also spotlight the paradox of man—his insignificance when measured against the universe and his greatness when standing before God. So the psalmist, seeing man against the backdrop of the universe, queries, "What is man that thou art mindful of him. . . ? / Yet thou hast made him little less than God, / and dost crown him with glory and honor. / Thou hast given him dominion over the works of thy hands" (Ps. 8:4-6). There are two overarching questions about the chief actors in the stewardship drama of creation and redemption. One is, What is man? But that cannot be answered without asking, Who is God that he should be mindful of man?

In the Beginning, God—

Christian stewardship—the drama of life—begins with God and not man. The opening words of the Bible read, "In the beginning, God created the heavens and the earth" (Gen. 1:1). The God who is maker of the heavens and the earth is the very presupposition of all our thinking about life and the world. As a further way of defining who the creator God is, the New Testament speaks of Jesus Christ as God's agent of creation: "In the beginning was the Word, . . . and the Word was God. He was in the beginning with God" (John 1:1-2). But who is this God who creates through the Word, and what is there about him that would entitle him to claim absolute ownership over the world and man?

For one thing, in the beginning there is only God. *God is the only eternal or ultimate reality in the universe.* The Bible depicts God's repeated assertion, "For I am God, and there is no other" (Isa. 45:22). God alone is eternal and uncreated. Everything else in the universe is created and depends upon God for its existence. It is virtually impossible to imagine a time when the universe did not exist. And yet it is basic to Christian theology to think of a point beyond space and time when God was the only reality, when his own life was so absolute that there was not even preexistent matter or chaos, much less other gods, alongside himself.

God alone is the eternal God. The Bible describes his unique wholly otherness with terms like *Lord* and *Holy One.* Nothing within the created order can be compared to him. For that reason, as the only eternal and ultimate reality in the universe, God will tolerate no rivals, whether they be other gods, human beings pretending to be gods, or man's turning the universe itself into an idol. Man's whole life, values, and

31

ultimate concerns can properly be directed only to the sovereign eternal God of the universe. No wonder the psalmist asks, "Who is like the Lord our God?" (Ps. 113:5).

And what is this God-of-the-beginning like? Whatever he is, he is not a God who *needs* the world and therefore is forced to create. *The eternal God is a personal God of love who has within his own triune nature all that is necessary for him to be the eternal God who is sufficient within himself.* In describing God as personal love, we encounter the limitations of human language in trying to picture what God is within himself. We represent God with the symbols of the highest values and realities we experience in life. The highest of these is undoubtedly our personal life. From a theological perspective we may assume that God may be greater than personal as we understand it, but he is at least personal.

But for that very reason, some viewpoints might argue that it is contradictory to say that God is both personal love and self-sufficient. Love, it is argued, implies relationships that require at least two persons. If God is love, then he *must* create a world and persons to love. Or there is that classic moment in the great drama *Green Pastures,* when God rests in his eternal solitude and aloneness, musing about what to do. And finally he says: "I'm lonely. I'll make me a world."

At this point the Christian doctrine of the Trinity proves to be more than a theological curiosity. The idea of the triune God is of critical importance for affirming that the God of personal love is eternally self-sufficient and does not need the world in order to be a God of love. In the New Testament, God reveals himself as Father, Son, and Spirit. And different passages connect the Son and the Spirit with the Father in the divine creative activity. The creator God is a triune God. In the inner trinitarian personal life of God, he is an eternal community of love. The Father, Son, and Spirit give and receive love from all eternity. Although God must not be conceived of as three individuals, he is a personal God who in some sense is community within himself. The point for a theology of stewardship is this: God is so complete within himself that he does not *need* another reality—a world or a human being—in order to be a God of giving love.

So the question arises, Why did God create the world? And the answer is not, because he had to. *God creates the world out of sheer grace, not out of internal needs or external necessities.* Because of the completeness of God's inner trinitarian life, he does not need to create a world in order to fulfill his nature of love. Nor is God an unwilling victim of his own uncontrollable creative urges, so that the world becomes a necessary extension of his own divine life. Because God is the only ultimate reality, the world has not existed eternally alongside and over against God as a chaotic reality with which his creativity is fated to struggle. No, in a free act representing a creative choice, God creates a world outside himself.

The personal nature of God is the key to understanding his personal purposes in the universe. God's motivation in the creative process is to glorify himself in the creation of life outside himself and the sharing of himself with his intelligent creatures. As C. S. Lewis has memorably observed, God "is so brimful of existence that he can give existence away."[5] God's creative love, however, is gift love, not need love. We often speak of the grace of God in relation to redemption. But grace did not originate at Calvary. It reached out with God's decision to create a world and human life. Life itself is a gift from God. Merely to be alive and to struggle with the question of the meaning and purpose of life is pure gift. Out of grace the eternal divine love creates the world as the stage for the divine-human drama of redemption.

God Created the Heavens and the Earth

Genesis introduces the symphony of life with the refrain, "In the beginning God created the heavens and the earth" (Gen. 1:1). *God is the creator of all that exists, from the cosmos to man.* God is the absolute creator, sustainer, and sovereign lord of the universe. All things have their origin and purpose in his will. The New Testament pictures the divine creative activity taking place in and through Jesus Christ who is the agent and goal of creation. Paul asserts, "For in him all things were created, in heaven and on earth, . . . all things were created through him and for him. He is before all things, and in him all things hold together" (Col. 1:16-17). And John adds, "Without him was not anything made that was made" (John 1:3).

The Old Testament also stresses the absolute character of the divine creative act in the poetic magnificence of its great pictures of creation in passages like Genesis 1 and 2; Isaiah 50; Psalms 8, 19, and 104; and Job 38. These passages underline the uniqueness and incomparability of the divine creative act. The Hebrew word that is translated "to create" in Genesis 1:1 and in some other passages is *bara*. The word is used only for God's unique creative activity. Only God can *bara* the heavens and the earth. The word refers to a creative ordering of chaos so incomparable that it points toward an absolute creation. The dimensions of the creative act are so great that the holy transcendent God is the sovereign lord and ruler of the universe. The universe remains dependent upon God at every point. If for a moment God were to withdraw his creative power and will, the universe would collapse into chaos (see Pss. 88:13; 104:7-9).

Christian theology has traditionally pictured the absolute sovereignty of God over the creative process by the idea of creation out of nothing. The technical theological term is *creatio ex nihilo*. Creation out of nothing means that God did not create the world out of his own being so that the world is divine, or out of some primeval chaos eternally opposed to God. Creation out of nothing means that the universe is neither an eternal reality alongside God, a cosmic accident, nor a divine necessity. The creative process is an act of the divine will motivated by the divine love. God did not have to create. He freely chose to create and to share his love with a created world outside himself. The world has not always existed. What is, might not have been and once was not. The created order is absolutely dependent upon God for its origin and its continuation in existence.

As sovereign creator and lord, God is owner of everything in the universe, and he alone has the right to define the nature and purpose of life and the world he has made. The psalmist sings, "The earth is the Lord's and the fulness thereof, / the world and those who dwell therein; / for he has founded it" (Ps. 24:1-2). That is a declaration of the Creator's rights of ownership. Isaiah proclaims, "Thus says the Lord: 'Heaven is my throne / and the earth is my footstool' " (Isa. 66:1). The Creator alone can legitimately claim, "For every beast of the forest is mine, / the cattle on a thousand hills. / . . . For the world and all that is in it is mine" (Ps. 50:10-12).

The New Testament centers God's ownership of the universe in the creative *and* redemptive work of Jesus Christ. Creation itself is viewed through the redemption in Christ. In fact, the very purpose of creation is the goal of reconciliation of the world to God through his mighty act in Jesus Christ. The goal and purpose of creation is actualized and made possible through the incarnation of God in Christ. "For in him all the fulness of God was pleased to dwell," Paul writes, "and through him to reconcile to himself all things, whether on earth or in heaven, making peace by the blood of his cross" (Col. 1:19-20). God is sovereign lord and owner of creation in the twofold sense that he has both created and redeemed all things in and through Jesus Christ.

Man the Steward

The universe exists as a theater for the glory of God. "The heavens are telling the glory of God," sings the psalmist, "and the firmament proclaims his handiwork" (Ps. 19:1). The physical universe itself is a magnificent creative achievement. When man measures himself against the vastness of the universe, he is insignificant in his own eyes but, oddly enough, not in the eyes of God. "When I look at thy heavens, / . . . what is man that *thou* art mindful of him?" (Ps. 8:3-4; emphasis added). In the divine scheme of things,

35

no matter how spectacular and dazzling this universe of God's, without man there is still an emptiness in the theater.

What is man? Only a creature so important that the psalmist can say, "Thou hast made him little less than God" (Ps. 8:5). Had God stopped his creative process short of producing man, he might have been a grand architect or an incomparable cosmic artist, but not the God he actually is—the master of the divine art of person-making. Incredible as it seems, in God's estimate man is the most important thing in the universe. What is there about man that so captures God's attention? What is there about his nature and position in the creative process that inclines the psalmist to describe him as "little less than God"? A theology of stewardship must know who God is, but it also must know who man is.

And God Made Man in His Own Image

The universe is complete and the glory of God fulfilled only when the human actor walks upon the stage. Then the universe becomes a cosmic theater where God can manifest his presence and give himself to man in a divine-human venture. As the crowning achievement of God's creative work, man can witness to the glory of God and enter into personal relationships with his Creator. From the first instant of creation the whole process has been geared to producing human beings who embody personal life and are capable of love and relationships with God and man.

Man is the focal point of God's personal purposes in creation and redemption. The Genesis 1 creation story describes the creative acts of God as they move to a climax on the sixth day of creation when God makes man in his own image. And at each stage of the process, God observes, "It is good." But, finally, after who knows how many billions of years, man emerges from the process. Then with man on the scene, God surveyed his creation; and suddenly the galaxies, stars, planets, and lower forms of life took on new meaning. So at the end of the sixth day, with man standing in the midst of the world, the story relates, "God saw everything that he had made, and behold, it was very good" (Gen. 1:31). In the stewardship drama, the human actor has entered the play and the divine-human venture begins.

As the focal point of creation, man is uniquely the creature of God, the one species of creaturely life that bears the image of God himself. What is man? He is made in the image *of* God. He is the creature of God. He cannot be defined apart from God. He alone of all the creatures knows God in personal relationship. He can not only be loved by God but also love God in return. To be man as God intended, man must live in relation to and for God.

As the creature made in the image of God, man is a unique in-between creature, a created being who exists somewhere between the Creator and creatures and who is related to both. As a creature, man is—unlike God—related to the whole chain of created life. In Genesis 2 and 3 he is called a creature of dust, biologically one with all living creatures (see Gen. 2:7). And yet man is also distinct from the rest of the created beings on earth. As the one who bears the image of God, he is uniquely related to God.

The image of God is a complex symbol used of no other creature. It indicates that man has a unique relationship and responsibility to God. Man is made for fellowship with God and obedience to his will. But as image-bearer, man also represents God on the face of the earth. He is God's vice-regent, the rational, responsible creature who in communion and cooperation with God shares in God's work in the world. And as steward, man bears a unique responsibility and accountability to God in the created order.

As the creature made in the image of God, man is capable of living in a personal relationship with his Creator and with his fellow human beings, reflecting at the creaturely level a created likeness to the personal nature of the eternal God of love. What is God like? It helps to remember that he is a triune God. Although we cannot perfectly comprehend the personal nature of God or clearly picture the triune inner life of God, we know enough to be certain that if man is made in the image of God, he is made for personal existence. And the doctrine of the Trinity teaches us that personhood and love can never be attained apart from community and relationships.

It is not surprising, then, that the image of God as described in Genesis 1 is a social image. Man is not created as an isolated individual but as a human community. The Hebrew word translated "man" in Genesis 1 is *adham*, which means "mankind." God says, "Let us make man in our image, after our likeness; and let *them* have dominion. . . . So God created man in his own image, in the image of God he created him; male and female he created them" (Gen. 1:26-27; emphasis added). Similarly, the older creation story of Genesis 2 emphasizes in its own style that man is fully man only when man and woman stand before each other (see Gen. 2:23-24). Male and female are a symbol for every human community, for man's existence before God as a social being.

God himself, astonishingly, desires personal relationships with his human subjects. Because they mirror his own life on earth, he also wills personal relationships within human communities. And one cannot be fully had without the other. That is the whole purpose of creation and redemption. And so the great commandment: "You shall love the Lord your God with all your heart, . . . and your neighbor as yourself" (Luke 10:27). That commandment is the heart of Christian stewardship!

It is risky business for God to open himself to personal relationships with his human creatures. *Freedom and responsibility within man's creaturely limits are essential elements in human personal life.* Personal relationships occur only when they are freely entered. Love cannot be coerced. So personal relationships require freedom. And that is the problem! Freedom can be misused. Man's freedom *for* God can be twisted into freedom *from* God. God makes man responsible for his use or misuse of freedom. A proper use of freedom requires a sense of responsibility to do God's will within the limits of our creaturely life. Man is meant for God. But man must freely and responsibly choose to love and serve God. So God took the risk, knowing that a person, even one misusing his freedom, is better than a puppet.

The Genesis creation stories vividly portray the freedom and creaturely limitations of man in the divine plan. In the Genesis 1 story, man is given dominion over all living things and is to fill and subdue the earth (see Gen. 1:26-28). In the Genesis 2 story, God puts man in the Garden to till the ground and to name the animals. He receives no hint in either story about how to exercise dominion or what to call the animals. Man is not a robot. His personal life before God requires freedom.

And yet, man is not absolutely free. Man is free to choose how he will live, but he exercises that freedom within the limits of his own creaturely finitude. Man is free to be man. He is not free to be God. In his freedom he is responsible for living his life according to the will and purpose of God. The Genesis stories portray what it means to live in responsible freedom. Man has a delegated authority. God *commands* man to have dominion over the earth. And although man exercises his dominion in freedom, he finally remains responsible to God for how he uses his freedom. In the story of the garden of Eden, Adam and Eve have free run of the garden—almost. There is one exception. They must not eat of the tree of the knowledge of good and evil (see Gen. 3:1-3). This symbolic prohibition sets the creaturely limits of man's freedom. Man may be God's representative in ruling the earth, but he is not God. The prohibition of the tree reminds man that he is a creature, a steward, who remains responsible to his Creator.

And God Gave Man Dominion

In the words of the psalmist, "Thou hast given him dominion over the works of thy hands; / thou hast put all things under his feet" (Ps. 8:6). *Man's role in life is to glorify God by loving God and man and by exercising dominion in God's world, by acting as God's representative in the created order, living*

39

creatively in the authority delegated from God, and finally by being responsible to God for actions in his life. Man alone of all the creatures can rise above nature and direct it. He alone is not dominated by instinct and adaptive behavior. As bearer of the image of God, man can be God's managerial representative on earth.

God places the world under man's management. And that management takes place in responsible freedom. In the Genesis stories, God gives man a general command to manage the earth. Man is to fill, subdue, have dominion, till, and name. That is, he is to become an active participant in God's own work of creation. In a figurative sense, God makes man a junior partner in the creative process. This mutual divine-human venture into a creative future provides the dynamic, power, and goal of the life of stewardship. Man's stewardship over the earth involves him in a creative collaboration with God in God's own creative process.

Man's responsibility to God includes his corporate human relationships as well as those of his individual life. The image of God in Genesis 1 is a corporate image. Man bears that image only in community. The command to exercise dominion in the earth is given to mankind, not merely to individuals (see Gen. 1:26-31). And the redemptive work of God reflects his intention in creation and is directed toward bringing man into a redeemed community of faith through the old covenant with Israel and the new covenant with the church (see Heb. 8:6; 12:24).

The implication is unmistakable for the Christian stewardship of life. Stewardship is not merely the individual's responsibility for his own life. It includes his social responsibility for the resources and created values of the whole world as he participates at every level of society. Man—both as an individual and as a member of human communities—is ultimately accountable to God for how he lives out his personal relationships with God and man and exercises his own creative responsibility to manage the resources of life.

And by One Man Came Life

What is man? Little less than God! True. But he is also the creature who tries to play God. The glory of man before his Maker underscores the tragedy of man when separated from his Maker. Man is a sinner who misuses his freedom to become a rebel against God, to turn from worshiping and serving the Creator to worshiping the creature and the creation. The result is that man has lost clear and adequate knowledge of God and of the ultimate meaning of life (see Rom. 1:18-32). We are made for personal relationships with our Creator but use our freedom to declare our independence from God. We are made to live in love with our fellow human beings, but history is the story of human conflicts and inhumanity to man. We are made for creative management of life's resources, but we misuse the gift of life and abuse God's world.

As a responsible steward, man cannot reject God's ownership of the universe and get away with it. Man remains accountable to God—even if he refuses to recognize God's place as lord of his life. Genesis pictures man being cast out of the Garden and barred from returning in his own natural strengths and capacities (see Gen. 3:22-24).

And yet, God does not give man up! God has rights of ownership. He holds title to our lives. And he pursues his divine right with the weapon of love, even in the face of our opposition. Man must marvel at the grand madness of the Creator—to associate with creatures like ourselves, to suffer the pain of rejection, to endure the agony of pursuing us as a hound of heaven, to accept the humiliation of watching the creature pretend to be his own creator.

"For the wages of sin is death," says Paul, "but the free gift of God is eternal life in Christ Jesus our Lord" (Rom. 6:23). In a key text for stewardship, Paul writes that "one man's act of righteousness leads to acquittal and life for all men" (Rom. 5:18). How are we to understand that? Jesus Christ makes Christian stewardship possible! Jesus not only most perfectly

41

reveals the meaning of Christian stewardship, but his redemptive act makes it attainable. According to Paul, Jesus embodies the perfect image of God, and those in Christ increasingly appropriate that image, the new nature, in the life of faith (see Col. 3:10). *The Christian begins the recovery of the full image of God and of authentic humanity in a saving encounter with God through faith in Jesus Christ and the consequent life of Christian discipleship lived within the fellowship of the church and in service to the world.*

God's redemptive action in Christ was no afterthought. It is not as if man's sin caught God by surprise. In his eternal wisdom, God knew what man would do with his freedom and knew the great cost of his redemption. Ephesians declares that "he chose us in him before the foundation of the world" (Eph. 1:4). In a mystifying sense, the cross was eternally in the heart of God. Creation and redemption go hand in hand. The grace that gives us life is the grace that makes possible the new life. The gospel is that "God so loved the world that he gave his only Son" (John 3:16). Only when I realize that great cost of my redemption do I envision the nobility of my own human potential in the great venture with God in Christian stewardship.

God's purpose in creation, then, is bound up with his redemptive purpose in Jesus Christ. God's creative activity extends into the redemptive reality of the new creation that grows out of the incarnation of God in Christ and moves the universe toward its goal of final transformation at the end of history (see II Cor. 5:17; I Tim. 6:15). The final goal of creation is that new creation when God will live in fellowship with the redeemed of all the ages in an eternal giving and receiving of love. The eternal community of personal relationships between the personal God and the community of the redeemed in Jesus Christ is the ultimate goal of all creation. And all the processes of life and of the church must facilitate this personal purpose of God. That is the divine-human drama of stewardship.

III
The World as a Stage

"All the world's a stage, / And all the men and women merely players," wrote Shakespeare (*As You Like It*). In a profound theological sense, that is correct. The world is the stage for the drama of stewardship in which God is the owner and man the steward. The world is the estate over which man exercises stewardship. The personal relationships between God and man are acted out in the world and involve man's dominion in the earth as God's representative over it. Therefore, a theologically informed view of responsible Christian stewardship requires that we have a clear understanding of the nature and purpose of the world in the plan of God and of how man is to view and live in the world as a responsible steward.

One's view of the world will powerfully shape the character and style of one's Christian stewardship. So a critical stewardship question is: What is the nature of the world? Is it good or evil or a bit of both? The Christian understanding is complex. The Christian view rejects a pessimistic view that regards the world as so inherently evil that our salvation task is basically to escape from it. On the other hand, the Christian view rejects an optimistic view that disregards the evil and sin in the world and leads one to value the world as the ultimate reality.

The Uniqueness of the Christian World View

The Christian view of the world is somewhat unique among world views. It rejects a number of widely held viewpoints in the contemporary world. For example, there is the Gnostic-Manichaean view that the world is evil and that salvation consists in separating spirit from matter. It might even be stated in exaggerated eschatologies within the Christian Church. Its motto is "Stop the world, I want to get off." It views the world with disdain or even hatred. But the Christian rejects such a negative reading of the world and affirms that this is the Father's world. Despite a frank recognition of the evil and sin in the world, the Christian faith affirms the intrinsic goodness and value of the world.

The Christian view rejects another widely held view found particularly within Eastern religions. Among some forms of Hinduism, the world is viewed as transitory and harmful to man's ultimate goal of escaping the wheel of existence and returning to Nirvana. Or, in some forms of Buddhism, the world is viewed as unreal and illusory, so that wisdom is to be detached from the world. But the Christian faith views the world as substantial and real, and its value as so great that it will be finally transformed into a new heavens and a new earth, being taken up into the eternal purposes of God.

A third pervasive view is so obsessed with the value of the world that the world becomes an end in itself. Marxists and some capitalists affirm that the world itself is man's ultimate value and that the acquisition of material things is the highest good in life. But the Christian faith views the world within the eternal purposes of God, so that the world can never be allowed to become an end in itself, no matter what kind of value we attach to it. The world is the instrument of God's purposes and must not become an idol before which man bows.

The Christian view of the world is complex and paradoxical in comparison with most major alternative world views. It values the world without regarding the world as the ultimate value. It recognizes the evil in the world without allowing evil to have the final word. Although it recognizes the evil fractures in the world, the Christian view continues to affirm the reality, value, and intrinsic goodness of the world, its centrality in the purposes of God, and man's responsibility as a steward in God's world. The complex Christian understanding demands that the world be seen in its original goodness, its fallenness, its justification in Christ, and its future transformation. Only in that light can one begin to make sense of the New Testament's paradoxical demands that the Christian is to live in the world but not of the world (see John 17). In a striking way, the quality of Christian stewardship depends largely upon how one comes to terms with the nature of the world and chooses to live in it.

The Nature of the World

The complexity of the Christian world view is evidenced by the different terms the New Testament uses for the world and the varied meanings of some of the terms. The Greek term *oikoumene* normally refers to the physical world. When used in this sense for God's created order, the New Testament regards the world as intrinsically good. The word *aion,* usually translated "age," is sometimes used to contrast the present evil age with the life of the age to come. The third word is *kosmos,* which is often translated "world" or "universe." *Kosmos* can vary widely in its meaning, referring at times to the whole universe, the planet, the people, the world at enmity with God, or the world God loved and sought to redeem. Some of the confusion within the Christian Church about how we should view the world is perhaps a result of not maintaining the careful distinctions in the varied usages of the term.[6]

The terms *aion* and *kosmos* have two major diverse applications that are particularly important for understanding the nature of the world and man's stewardship in it. The words can refer quite literally to the physical order of creation, the world of nature in which God's purposes are worked out. Here God expects man to exercise dominion over the world and not to become dominated by or subjected

45

to the world. Evil has disrupted the harmony of the physical world, so that the world itself has a way of seducing human beings. Man can begin to worship the things of the world and become bound by the creation itself.

A second distinct meaning of the two words relates to the spiritual drama that is being enacted upon the physical order. In this sense, the world is the realm of God's reign, the world where the kingdom of God is being challenged by the kingdom of evil. The world of spiritual conflict is the fallen world where time, finite objects and values, and egocentric human capacities, aspirations, and purposes are deified. Here man worships the creature and creaturely values rather than the Creator. The fallen world does deserve a negative judgment. It is unreal, transitory, and illusory. It is in this sense that man is not to love the world or the things of the world. Injunctions against the love of the world or of conformity to the world are found particularly in the writings of John and Paul. Paul connects the "works of the flesh" with the values of the fallen world (see Gal. 5:16-24).

This complex attitude toward the world can best be comprehended within the framework of creation and redemption. Only in that context can we grasp how the universe can be intrinsically good and valuable and at the same time fractured by the reality of sin and evil.

The Original Goodness of the Created Order

The world was originally created good, and it evoked pleasure in its Creator as a perfect expression of his creative will and activity. The great creation stories of the Bible emphasize that fact. In the Genesis 1 story of creation, God calls his handiwork "good" at the end of each of the first five days of creation. Then at the end of the sixth day, when man stands on earth as the crowning achievement of creation, God surveys the world and calls it "very good." The original goodness is symbolized by the garden of Eden, the environment where everything is made for the well-being and joy of man, and man and animals live together in peace.

The Hebrew word *Eden* means "delight, happiness, or bliss" (see Gen. 2–3).

Out of this theological conviction, the Hebrews developed a healthy, world-affirming faith. As a creature made in the image of God, the Hebrew, like God himself, viewed the creation as good. He marveled at its mystery and grandeur, and rejoiced in all its earthly diversity. No Gnostic or Manichaean dualism with its negative view of the world can be found in the Old Testament. The world is God's good creation. All life has sanctity. There is no compartmentalization of life into the sacred and the secular. The Hebrew could never concentrate his interest on some limited spiritual sphere of life in isolation from the whole sweep of earthly existence. Everything comes from God.

Hebrew stewardship responsibility was inclusive of this present life, the natural world, and all created things that God has called good. God has a purpose for *this* world and for *this* life. For that reason, observes Walther Eichrodt, the Hebrew exulted in natural and cultural goods "of earthly possessions, many children, long life, friendship and love, as well as wisdom, beauty, honour and political freedom."[7]

The New Testament shares the Hebrew belief in the original goodness of creation. Understanding the Son of God to be the agent of creation, the apostles taught that "all things were made through him, and without him was not anything made that was made" (John 1:3). Therefore all created things are good, and they must be misused in order to be bad. A recurrent New Testament principle is: "For everything created by God is good" (I Tim. 4:4).

The Fallenness of the Created World

The question arises: Is our present world the world God originally created good? The answer is yes and no. It is still God's world, but the original goodness of the created order has been permeated, perverted, and fractured by evil and sin. That disruption is in the structure of the world, the order of nature, the species and realm of natural things, the

47

constitution of man himself, and in all man's social relationships (see Gen. 1–9; Rom. 1–8).

The Bible has several pictures of how evil enters the world. The most familiar is the Genesis 2 and 3 picture of Adam and Eve's being tempted by the serpent, attempting to usurp the place of God and to exercise their freedom beyond the limits of their responsibility to God, and trying finally to avoid accountability. The Old Testament consistently portrays evil as a stranger, an intruder in the world. Evil in some way represents good that has gone wrong. Evil is a parasite on the good and cannot sustain its own existence apart from leeching on the good.

The New Testament shares the conviction that evil is not a native in God's good universe. Evil represents the rebellion of a part of God's creation against the Creator himself. The conflict between good and evil is something like a civil war. The New Testament pictures sin and evil with a stark realism. Evil is alive and active, a subverting force in the creation and in human life. John describes it as the kingdom of darkness (see John 1:5; 3:19). Paul paints it with varied imagery, including describing it as "principalities, . . . powers, . . . world rulers, . . . spiritual hosts of wickedness in the heavenly places" (Eph. 6:12).

The seductive power and attraction of evil subverts man's responsible life before God. It leads him to worship and serve the creature rather than the Creator (see Rom. 1) and to love darkness rather than light (see John 1). It causes man to view the world as an end in itself and to lose the transcendent dimension of life. So Jesus warns, "Do not lay up for yourselves treasures on earth" (Matt. 6:19). Because of man's misuse of freedom, he begins to pursue life "after the flesh" (Rom. 8:5), that is, life whose values and purposes are separated from the purposes of God. Sin leads to the disruptions in society—to injustice, inequality, alienation, and to racial, class, and national divisions.

The divine response to man's rebellion is judgment. Man is responsible and reaps what he sows. The consequences of sin are graphically pictured in the Garden story of Genesis 3. Adam's sin brought a curse upon man and the world. The ground is accursed, work becomes exertion, and animals become hostile. Thorns and thistles spring up among plant life. Man is cast out of the Garden, from which he is barred by a flaming sword (see Gen. 3:14-24).

The New Testament also views the world as having fallen from its original state. It speaks in negative terms about the fallen world, contrasting the kingdoms of this world with the kingdom of God, and darkness with the divine light. Paul indicates "that the creation was subjected to futility" (see Rom. 8:18-23). He speaks of the "god of this world" who "has blinded the minds of the unbelievers" (II Cor. 4:4). In other places he refers to the "rulers of this age" (I Cor. 2:6) and "the world rulers of this present darkness" (Eph. 6:12). When John refers to this world, he often means "this present fallen age" that is "in the power of the evil one" (see John 12:31 and I John 5:19). He contrasts "this world" with "the world to come" (John 8:23, et al.). When Paul condemns "worldly passions," he has in mind the values of the fallen world (see Titus 2:12). Having fallen into decay and bondage, the creation now groans in travail, waiting "with eager longing for the revealing of the sons of God" (see Rom. 8:18-23).

The world remains intrinsically good, despite its fallenness. In biblical faith, there is no trace of a negative or pessimistic view of the world of matter. Biblical thought does not conceive of salvation as release from the tomb of the body or the prison of the material world. The Hebrews had a healthy, affirming, this-worldly faith. Life was for them a celebration of the delights of the created order and was to be enjoyed in all its pleasurable dimensions. All life is God's gift and, when lived in accordance with his intention, is good.

In New Testament thought, too, the world continues to have significance for both God and man. The Christian faith may condemn man's subservience to the value system of the fallen world, but it affirms the world as such. Jesus himself plunged into the whole sweep of life and affirmed it by

49

participating in it. Paul condemned those with overactive consciences who advocated renunciation of the world for an ascetic life-style of refusing marriage, engaging in self-abasement, and abstaining from foods. Paul's attitude toward the created order is unqualified: "For everything created by God is good, and nothing is to be rejected if it is received with thanksgiving" (I Tim. 4:4; see Mark 7:19; Col. 2:16; et al.).

The Redemption of the World

God's mighty act of redemption in Christ sets our perspective of even the fallen world in a new light. The gospel is: "In Christ God was reconciling the world to himself" (II Cor. 5:19). It is precisely the world that is at enmity with God that God embraces in the act of redemption. John unforgettably expresses it: "For God so loved *the world* that he gave his only Son, that whoever believes in him should not perish but have eternal life" (John 3:16; emphasis added). That redemption is on a cosmic scale, one in which God is redeeming the whole creative process. So we do not miss the point, Paul specifically says that in Christ God acted "to reconcile to himself all things, whether on earth or in heaven" (Col. 1:20).

The world is God's by right of creation and by right of redemption. For the Hebrews the redemption of the world was a hope of what was to come. They hoped for a day when God will recreate the world with order, peace, and fertility as he originally intended the world to be. They hoped for a restored human community, a renovated nature, a golden age, a new covenant, a new heavens and a new earth—a time when man could enjoy a long life free from the ancient problems that perplex the human family. Their hope was directed to this world where the new creation would fulfill the old creation. They hoped for the redemption of *this* world.

In a similar way, salvation in the New Testament is not primarily concerned to get people out of this world. Rather, the reconciliation of the world in Christ will eventuate in the future transformation of the world (see Rom. 8:21). What was set loose in the life, death, and resurrection of Christ was the life of the age to come. The powers of the future kingdom of God have been unleashed into the historical process. What the Hebrews hoped for has begun in Jesus Christ. So the future transformation of the universe is assured, although it has not yet occurred. The kingdom of God is still in conflict with the kingdom of darkness. The Christian lives in the dialectical tension between life in this present age and the claims of life in the age to come.

The Christian walks a razor's edge in being called to value the world, but not to value it too much, to affirm its intrinsic goodness without ignoring its evil, to recognize its evil without denying its goodness. He cannot despise the world because the world is being redeemed and will be ultimately transformed. On the other hand, he cannot treat the world as an ultimate value precisely because the world is in the process of being redeemed but is yet pervaded by evil.

Dietrich Bonhoeffer spoke of the world as having a penultimate value.[8] A penultimate value is the value before the final or ultimate value. What is ultimate is that future goal toward which the world and all the redeemed move, that event symbolized by the coming of Christ and the final judgment and beyond. This present world has value to that future point of transformation. If for no other reason, God sustains and preserves the world for the coming of Christ. Consequently, the Christian neither deifies nor disparages the world. The world has great value, but it is only penultimate value. The Christian cannot so exclusively look toward his future transformation that he renounces responsibility for the world. And yet, he cannot absolutize the world as though the world is the final value. The world that is being redeemed continues to be fractured by the conflict between good and evil.

The Future Transformation of the World

Many Christians have missed the cosmic dimensions of salvation, partly because of their preoccupation with

51

individual salvation. But in biblical thought the earth itself shares in man's estrangement from God, so that redemption involves the created order itself. The universe is also awaiting that day when the creative and redemptive purposes of God will be accomplished in fullness.

The Hebrew hope for the future restoration of the Hebrew nation involved a transformed nature. Old Testament writings are full of those idealized pictures of hills lowered and valleys raised, of lion and lamb lying down together, of a river of healing waters bringing life to the arid desert. Isaiah graphically describes how out of the final chaos God will recreate a new heaven and a new earth that surpass the old creation (see Isa. 65:17; 66:22).

The New Testament hope for the transformation of the universe is colored by the hope for the resurrection of the dead (see I Thess. 4:13; I Cor. 15). As is the resurrection of the body, the future transformation of the universe is unimaginable. It will preserve the value and earthly reality of the cosmic process but transform it into a new dimension. Along with the redemption of Christians, the redemption of the cosmos has already begun and is in process. In terms that virtually defy our modern understanding, Paul depicts the universe groaning and travailing in the birth pangs of its future transformation, looking expectantly and straining forward to its future redemption and awaiting the revealing of the sons of God (see Rom. 8:19).

There is a concreteness of this New Testament expectation that prohibits any rarefied spiritual understanding of redemption. Redemption encompasses the very stuff of our earthly existence. Paul spells out that all things on earth have been reconciled to God through Christ (see Col. 1:20). God's plan for the fullness of time is "to unite all things in him, things in heaven and things on earth" (Eph. 1:10). The book of Revelation vividly sums up this hope for the transformation of the universe when it describes the heavens being rolled up like a scroll, the mountains and islands being displaced, and a new heavens and a new earth coming down out of heaven to earth (see Rev. 6:14; 21:1). What that future transformation will be like is unthinkable. But what is thinkable is the intrinsic value and redeemed potential of the world that will be ultimately transformed. This historical stage for the drama of creation and redemption will be taken up and transformed into the eternal stage for the eternal drama of the life of man in union with the Creator and Redeemer.

The Purpose of the World

If nature shares in man's fall, redemption, and future transformation, how should we understand its purpose in the divine-human drama? Several values should be noted. For one thing, the universe gives pleasure to God himself. The universe is a canvas revealing the creative artistry of God. The Genesis writer in chapter 1 magnificently portrays the divine pleasure over the creative process. Man is the crowning glory, but the creation has significance to God in and of itself. The Wisdom tradition of the Old Testament and many of the psalms celebrate the mighty creative works of God, which represent his wisdom in action. God pleasures himself in the beauty of his universe.

The world, secondly, is instrumental to the divine purposes in creation and redemption. In the context of stewardship, it is the estate over which the owner sets his steward. It is in the world that man must live in responsible freedom, managing the resources of the Creator in accordance with his creative purposes and, finally, standing accountable for his management. It is the divine laboratory for the human experiment in person-making, the environment in which the divine-human relationship is acted out, the testing ground for human growth. And in that sense, the universe is the stage for the stewardship drama.

Third, the world is basic to human survival. Man bears the image of God, but man also stands in continuity with the whole chemical and biological creative process. Genesis 2 portrays man being made out of the dust of the earth and being brought to life by the inbreathing of spirit, so that he is quite literally earth man (see Gen. 2:7). Man has certain survival needs, just as any other living organism. These include such elemental values as food, water, housing, and clothing, which are never demeaned or minimized in biblical thought (see Matt. 6). But man is more than a biological organism. He is mind, spirit, the image of God. His needs are more than physical. And so the mystery of the universe arouses his deepest longings about the meaning and purpose of life (see Pss. 8, 104). The beauty of the universe satisfies man's need to experience beauty, to wonder at the intricacies of living things, to imbibe the panorama of the universe. The universe is even a spiritual instrument of God that in its incredible harmony and beauty draws man's mind to God.

All these are critical dimensions in man's survival as man, of his standing above the level of animals. The universe is instrumental to distinctive human existence itself. Not the least, the world is the common environment that makes love possible between two human beings. In our earthiness, we leave parents and cleave to one another in organic union (see Gen. 2:24). The earth makes possible the formation of human communities that are integral to human fulfillment and happiness.

Fourth, the world provides a sphere for human dominion, work, and creative activity. The biblical writings stress the centrality in human life of man's dominion over the natural world. Genesis 1 tells how God commanded man to be fruitful and multiply, to fill and subdue the earth, and to have dominion over all living things (see Gen. 1:28-30). Genesis 2 describes how God put man in the garden of Eden to till and keep it and to rule over the animal order. Man is free under God to shape the natural world, to build his cultures, and to create his technologies. Such a role is essential to man's creative fulfillment. But man's role of dominion can lead to

54

tragedy when God's representative on earth begins to think that he himself is God. Yet as long as he remains responsible to God, man is open to a creative future. He can live as an active participant in God's own creative process. In the next chapter, we will consider the role of man in God's world.

IV
Man in God's World

Man is a steward in God's world, both as an individual and as a member of the human family. His task is to manage every facet of life—his personal gifts and resources and the world's resources—in the service of God's purposes in creation and redemption. Those purposes focus upon man's personal existence in relationships with God and man. The world is instrumental to God's personal intentions. In consistency with God's personal purposes, man exercises his stewardship in freedom, responsibility, and accountability before God. Although man shares in corporate stewardship in his human communities, stewardship responsibility ultimately falls upon the individual. Only the individual can use his responsible freedom to respond to God in faith and to participate in the personal and social processes that manage the stewardship spheres of nature and history.

Stewardship responsibility includes one's sphere of private life and his spheres of corporate life in the world of nature and the processes of history. Each individual has personal gifts and spheres of responsibility that are unique to him as a distinctive person before God. In his individual role, he is responsible for such gifts of God as the limited time allotted to his life, his natural and spiritual abilities and capacities, his own immediate personal relationships, his material resources, and his redemptive Christian responsibilities as a servant of Christ and member of the church.

The individual is also responsible for a wide range of social resources and spheres of life that are entrusted to the whole human family. Christian theology has often expressed this human responsibility in and for the world by speaking of the orders of creation within which man is destined to live. God builds certain structures into human society that are designed for its stability and continuity, such as marriage and family, labor and culture, and government—the gifts of creation.

All human beings, not only Christians, are accountable to God for their stewardship of life. The Bible is clear in stating that all people share alike in the providential care of God. God gives life to everyone and allots them their place on earth in order that they might seek and find him (see Acts 17:24-28). Even after man's expulsion from the garden of Eden, God holds him accountable (see Gen. 4–9). After the Flood, God again charges fallen mankind to exercise dominion over the earth and to be accountable for how they fulfill that trust (see Gen. 9). Above all, fallen man still bears the image of God in exercising his responsibility within nature and history. Paul indicates that the Law is written on the hearts of the Gentiles and that both Jew and Gentile are accountable to God for their response to the degree of revelation they have (see Rom. 2).

The implications for this broader human responsibility are critical for our modern secular world where Christians are a minority. All people have a stewardship responsibility within the natural order and in history—even if they are not aware of the gifts and responsibilities of redemption and are fallen stewards in a fallen world. Yet here is the only real basis for our common human effort to manage the resources of the modern world—in politics, economics, ecology, and the varied desperate human needs of our time.

Redemption, however, places new and higher demands upon the Christian as he lives out his life in the world. If one confesses faith in Jesus Christ, he becomes responsible for the gifts of redemption and, consequently, in a more demanding way for the gifts of creation. He is let in on the secret meaning of the stewardship drama (see Eph. 3:1-13). He discovers who is the owner of the universe and the master of life and what God is about in creation and redemption. He is redeemed into a stewardship community (see I Pet. 4:10), the family of God, that embodies the new kind of personal life and is entrusted with spreading it to the rest of the world.

The Christian is also liberated in Christ to live a joyful, free, responsible, truly human life before God in God's good creation. The Christian steward is called to live in the world but not of the world (see John 17:11-19). The Christian faith does not take us out of the world but returns us to the world to live in single-minded awareness of God and in intimate acquaintance with the world. The Christian sees the world through new eyes, discovers new values in it, and lives in it with a higher sense of stewardship responsibility over the gifts of creation and redemption. He lives in conscious awareness of his ultimate accountability to Jesus Christ as lord. Of these persons Jesus says in a stewardship parable, "Blessed are those servants whom the master finds awake when he comes" (Luke 12:37).

The Christian, then, is steward of the gifts of creation and redemption—the whole of life itself. For the sake of clarity and manageability within a brief space, we will discuss in this chapter the individual's stewardship of his individual gifts, including time, natural and spiritual capacities and abilities, personal relationships, and the corporate stewardship responsibilities within the orders of creation—marriage and family, labor, and government. Because of their critical importance and popular interest to the practice of Christian stewardship, we will reserve separate chapters for the stewardship of material resources and the stewardship of the church.

The Stewardship of Individual Resources

The Christian steward is not just man in general but a particular individual with a specific name. He is born into a certain family, nationality, and geographical setting with opportunities that are provided and limited by his unique role and place in the world. His stewardship responsibilities begin with those gifts and resources that are unique to his own existence as God's creature.

The Stewardship of Time

Christian stewardship is lived in a limited amount of time—and time is therefore a critical element. In the stewardship parables of Jesus, the master goes away for a time, during which the steward is responsible for managing his estate. When the master returns unexpectedly, the steward will be accountable for what he has accomplished in the master's absence (see Luke 12:41-48). The Bible poses a principle for the stewardship of time: "Look carefully then how you walk, not as unwise men but as wise, *making the most of the time,* because the days are evil. Therefore do not be foolish, but understand what the will of the Lord is" (Eph. 5:15-17; emphasis added).

Life is a continuing transition between the poles of birth and death. The steward's dilemma is that he does not know how many acts are in the stewardship drama or when the final curtain will drop. Death is the overriding prospect for man. We will die, and we do not know when! That unexpected end is a recurring note in the stewardship parables. "Fool," says Jesus. "This night your soul is required of you" (Luke 12:20). Death is a threat because it represents the cancellation of possibilities in life, the termination of achievement, the end of the routine process of living. And death is always there before us—as end, goal, and final judgment.

Thus the challenging question confronts the steward: How do I live life in the face of unpredictable death? That question should bring a sense of urgency, seriousness, contemplation, action, engagement to our lives. It sets time within the sweep of eternity. Because God broke into history and eternity into time in Jesus Christ, the Christian knows who is lord of time, what time is for, and what time it is (see Gal. 4:4). The Christian has discovered values that matter, the style of life that endures, the achievements that transcend time and are transposable into eternity, and what it means to live authentically and not merely to exist. He redeems the time.

The Stewardship of Natural and Spiritual Gifts

The Christian is responsible for his own personal capacities and abilities, the physical, mental, and spiritual gifts that enter into one's efforts toward responsible living and effective Christian service in the world. The Christian faith is wholistic and is therefore concerned with our bodily existence, our emotional and mental health, the use of our intelligence, our private and public conduct, our personal and social ethics, and the productive use of our natural and spiritual abilities.

Body. As a living soul, man is both body and spirit. Like other biological organisms, man's body is essential to life. His biological needs and functions that must be met include nourishment, exercise, rest, relaxation, sleep, and sex. The body is so vital to human existence that the biblical hope is for a future resurrection of a spiritual body before the redeemed enjoy the fullness of eternity (see I Cor. 15). The good steward will keep his physical organism functioning at peak efficiency through proper diet, exercise, rest and relaxation, adequate sleep, weight control, and intelligent health habits.

In urging care and discipline of the body, Paul calls the Christian's body the temple of God or of the Spirit (see Rom. 8:11). We are to glorify God in our bodies (see I Cor. 6:19-20) by presenting them as a living sacrifice to God (see Rom. 12:1). We are to discipline the body so that it is not put to dishonorable use or subjected to the fallen values of the world (see I Cor. 9:25, 27), which might include excesses in food or drink or improper sexual gratification. In Semitic hyperbole, Jesus stresses the importance of bodily discipline by saying we are to cut off the hand, foot, or eye if necessary for the sake of the Kingdom (see Mark 9:42-48).

Mind. The great commandment charges us to love God with the mind (see Luke 10:27). The mind partly distinguishes man from other animals. It is integral to obeying

God's command to manage the earth and to responding to the claims of the kingdom of God. The Christian should develop his intelligence to the limits of his own capacity and the opportunities available in his society. In a time of exploding scientific and technological knowledge, the Christian should utilize his intellectual gifts in the total pursuit of the knowledge that enriches life. That should include Christian education. Knowledge should lead to the wisdom that enables human beings to cope with the practical stuff of living, to know and do the will of God, to live as a responsible steward.

Conduct. Christian personal and social ethics are basic to Christian stewardship. We are to live a life worthy of our calling as Christians (see Eph. 4:1). We are "created in Christ Jesus for good works" (Eph. 2:10) and are to bear the fruit of the Spirit (see Gal. 5:22). Christians can become preoccupied with either personal or social ethics, to the neglect of the other. Some become obsessed with their private code of conduct and may forget about the comprehensive social ethic of the Christian faith—the need to work for justice and equality and to care for the poor and downtrodden of the world. At the opposite pole, some people with a sensitive social conscience and activist style may neglect the importance of personal behavior and morality. Christian stewardship insists that man is responsible for all his behavior—personally and socially, privately and publicly. Paul's motto is, "If we live by the Spirit, let us also walk by the Spirit" (Gal. 5:25).

Conversation. Words are powerful instruments. Jesus says, "I tell you, on the day of judgment men will render account for every careless word they utter" (Matt. 12:36). The tongue has an extraordinary capacity for good or evil. Words can scar a person's spirit, mar a reputation, broadcast gossip, or profane the most treasured things in life. Two of the Ten Commandments, on taking the name of God in vain and lying, are connected with the use of words (see Exod.

61

20:1-17). So Proverbs warns, "The perverse tongue will be cut off" (Prov. 10:31).

Words can also be creative instruments to speak truth, convey love, create poetry, express reality, and transmit the wisdom of the human race. Conversation has a way of laying bare the soul before the world. The Christian should use language to express the full range of his humanity and the joys of creation and redemption in love, laughter, sorrow, truth, beauty, even the gospel itself.

Influence. There are people in the contemporary scene who make selfishness a virtue, as though life were a private affair. A popular ethic would argue that anything is all right if it does not hurt anybody. But the Christian steward has a sphere of influence for which he is responsible. He must be conscious of how his life influences others for good or bad. Jesus warned about the consequences of a Christian's adverse influence: "Whoever causes one of these little ones who believe in me to sin, it would be better for him if a great millstone were hung round his neck and he were thrown into the sea" (Mark 9:42). More positively, Jesus urges, "Let your light so shine before men, that they may see your good works and give glory to your Father who is in heaven" (Matt. 5:16). Even more, Jesus says, "You shall be my witnesses" (Acts 1:8).

Abilities. The steward's abilities fall into two categories corresponding to creation and redemption. We have natural abilities we are born with and develop in the maturing process. They may be intelligence, technological skill, musical or other artistic ability, managerial qualities, personality, leadership gifts, manual abilities, or other skills. The Christian steward is responsible for discovering and developing his best aptitudes and abilities in ways that allow him through his vocation to make a maximum contribution to humanity and the present world, and not merely to make a living or to attain prominence or wealth.

The Christian also receives spiritual gifts that God confers on all members of the Body of Christ (see I Cor. 12:4-6). His gift is essential to the healthy functioning of the church and is to be used in the internal life of the church and in the church's ministry and mission in the world (see I Cor. 12:7; Rom. 12:6). First Peter 4:10 specifically links the steward's role with the use of his spiritual gift in the life of the church and in service to the world.

The Stewardship of Personal Relationships

The great commandment is to love God and to love our neighbor as ourselves (see Luke 10:27). If the central purpose of creation and redemption is person-making and has to do with personal relationships, then nothing is more important in Christian stewardship than what happens in our personal relationships that extend from our family to intimate groups to casual contacts in the larger society. Persons are the richest resource of our lives.

Beyond our family relationships, which are the most formative of all, there are various areas of primary and secondary personal relationships. Our responsibility is most intense in those primary social groups in which we have sustained relationships, face-to-face contact, and common interests. The groups may take shape at work, in social life, in the neighborhood, and certainly in the church. In our primary relationships we encounter the special people with whom we join together in mutually influencing—enriching or troubling—one another's growth toward mature personhood.

In these close relationships with people we know best, we learn how to open ourselves to others, to love and serve our neighbor as ourselves, to forgive and be forgiven, to help and be helped. In those primary relationships the Christian will never treat another human being as an object to be manipulated for his own benefit but always will relate to a person made in the image of God. Even in caring and effecting constructive growth in another, the Christian will never be more coercive than is God and will never infringe upon the integrity and sanctity of a friend's personhood. He will respect the freedom, responsibility, and accountability of each individual steward before God.

There are also secondary relationships in which we rub shoulders casually with people we really do not know, where relationships are more temporary, less intimate, less characterized by common interests. In the parable of the good Samaritan, Jesus indicates that our neighbor is even the person in need whom we casually encounter (see Luke 10:29-37). It matters how we affect people even in brief relationships. In such experiences, the Christian cannot usually provide sustained caring. But he can be a Christian presence to care, to love, to help, to be a reconciler, to affirm the worth of every human being.

Stewardship Within the Orders of Creation

The Christian has a responsibility for the world that remains out of the divine intention in creation. Living under the higher demands of redemption, he is responsible for participating as a human being in the structures of society that provide stability, order, and enrichment for the world. These orders of creation are spheres of practical obedience within the world where secular and sacred do not apply. They fall upon Christians and non-Christians alike. These orders are usually held to include marriage and family, labor, government, and the church. The church serves the redemptive purposes of God in the world and sets people free to live responsibly within the other orders.

Marriage and Family

Marriage and family compose the most important personal relationships we enjoy in life. Our most creative relationships ought rightly to occur within our family unit where marriage, the raising of children, and the care of one's parents take place. It is here that we most open ourselves to love and be loved in a mutual journey toward personal wholeness and fulfillment.

Jesus places great value on marriage and its sanctity (see Mark 10:2-12). Although he teaches that marriage is only an earthly phenomenon, it is an order of creation and the central institution of human society (see Mark 12:25). Both Genesis 1 and 2 describe how man and woman find fulfillment in each other. The good steward will select a marriage partner, if he marries, who complements his own person, shares his commitments and values, pledges lifelong fidelity with him, and facilitates their mutual development into authentic human beings who live as good stewards in God's world.

The stewardship of family includes careful family planning. Sex is a gift within marriage that is not to be used irresponsibly. In an era of exploding population, some form of family limitation is increasingly necessary. Although the Roman Catholic Church vigorously resists the use of artificial birth control devices, most Protestant churches sanction that as a means of family planning. Good stewardship would call for a family to limit children to the number it can provide for, and educate.

Family stewardship also requires the responsible rearing of children through providing for their basic physical, emotional, intellectual, and spiritual needs. Parental stewardship demands wisdom in aiding a child's developmental processes, so that love is mixed with discipline and freedom with authority. The family should be the primary school for personal development in which the child is raised toward responsible stewardship for his own adult life. That involves raising the child in the life of the church and providing Christian education. Parents should mix, appropriate to the age of the maturing child, the critical personal elements of freedom, responsibility, and accountability for behavior. Family stewardship calls upon children to honor their father and mother and calls upon parents to live so that they deserve such respect.

Family stewardship further involves care of one's parents

and other dependents. This obligation embraces far more than finances. It concerns caring, helping, and being present to aged parents. In our era when many people live extended years beyond retirement, sometimes in nursing homes, care and availability to their needs are vital to the health and well-being of the elderly and to Christian family stewardship. The early Christian Church made this a test of orthodoxy. Paul set a rule that still has application in modern society: "If any one does not provide for his relatives, and especially for his own family, he has disowned the faith and is worse than an unbeliever" (I Tim. 5:8).

Labor

Man's stewardship in the order of labor entails responsibility for things, values, and relationships, broadly involving property, culture, and society. The stewardship of labor grows out of God's command to fill, subdue, and exercise dominion over the earth (see Gen. 1:28). Adam is portrayed as being placed in the Garden to till and keep it (see Gen. 2:15). Work is integral to the divine purpose. Man creates at his level in reflection of God's own creative activity. The command to work remains after the fall of man in the Garden, although as a result of the Fall, man's work involves struggle, sweat, and agony (see Gen. 3:17-19). Under this mandate from God, man sustains his own life and creates things and values that contribute to the quality of human existence. The Christian steward will share his own personal load of his society's work whenever possible and make his own creative contribution to the whole of society.

In his corporate role in society, the Christian should advocate the necessity and nobility of work and urge society toward policies that employ all capable people in the productive economic output of society. At the same time, society must be humane and care for those who are unable to work because of planned unemployment, lack of skills, handicaps, parental obligations, or other problems. The state should deal creatively with human problems, using welfare for real needs and not for creating a class of professional nonworkers.

A major factor in today's stewardship of labor is the organizational revolution in modern technological-industrial societies. The majority of people are now employed in mass corporations in which the individual is easily dehumanized and turned into a computer number. The Christian steward should actively urge human concern and sensitivity upon the great corporations so that internal management processes deal with persons and not statistics. The steward might also help educate management and labor about the importance of equitable earnings for investor and worker alike.

The Christian steward might also attempt to influence corporations toward a wider social role. Several possibilities exist. Industry could take a new responsibility for vocational training of the unskilled and for retraining people whose skills are made obsolete by technological changes. Industry also should be urged both to conserve our limited natural resources and to protect the delicate ecological balance of our planet. Industry should also balance public and private needs so that the profit motive is always weighed against a product's long-term effect on the quality of life. And in a day of multinational corporations, management has worldwide stewardship obligations of equity and honesty toward the general public.

Government

Government is an order of creation ordained by God (see Rom. 13:1-17). It limits and brings order to the conflicting self-interests of its citizens, protects its citizens from the strong or enemies, and provides services that individuals alone cannot provide. Governmental leaders are servants of God (see Rom. 13:4). Much of the quality of life in the world is profoundly influenced by the political structures of a society.

As a citizen of two worlds, the Christian is called to exercise responsible citizenship within the state and to influence government to serve the purposes of God for the world. He has several obligations. (1) The Christian should support the order of government and pray for political rulers, even when politically in opposition to a particular ruling party, except in matters of strict conscience when the state attempts to usurp the place of God (see I Pet. 2:13; Rev. 13). (2) The Christian should willingly pay taxes to the state, which allow the state to serve the interests and needs of its citizens (see Rom. 13:6-7). (3) The Christian should actively participate in the political processes, particularly in a democratic state.

Several principles can be suggested for participatory political stewardship. (1) The Christian should be informed about candidates, political issues, and important legislation. (2) He should vote in democratic elections. (3) Some Christians ought to become political officeholders or governmental workers, to be the Christian presence in the political structures. (4) The Christian can also attempt to influence policies, legislation, and tax expenditures to serve human priorities and values—in health, education, welfare, justice and equality, the pursuit of peace, protection of the environment, and other human needs.

In our contemporary American culture, there are numerous pressing corporate concerns directly related to the nature of our personal existence before God. We will mention only a few. (1) Corporate society needs to bring full justice and equality to all citizens in our society, to eradicate the last barriers of race, ethnic origins, and sex to the enjoyment of the full privileges of American life. (2) Corporate stewardship must also not only care for the poor but seek to eliminate poverty from American life. In the United States, the poor are now locked into poverty pockets and groups. Christians should influence the state to adopt long-term policies that will lead to full employment and develop the poor and unskilled into productive members of society. (3) The preservation of our natural environment is critical. The government should limit the extravagant use of our natural resources and bring ecological sanity to our industrial processes and urban way of life. (4) Christians should influence the government to care for the enduring human concerns of welfare, the elderly, health, education, and other concerns that indicate the quality of life in any society. (5) The Christian should urge the government to pursue peace among the nations of the world. (6) The Christian should encourage the government to prevent the strong's taking advantage of the weak in economics.

Christian stewardship in the order of government should recognize the international role of governments in a world that has become a planetary neighborhood. Great social gaps exist among nations, especially between the technologically advanced countries and the underdeveloped countries. The world is fractured by tragic inequities. In a time when the Western states control a high percentage of the world's wealth, our corporate stewardship must call for the support of human rights in all nations, for equitable distribution of the world's raw materials and manufactured goods, and for eradication of poverty, disease, starvation, and ignorance from the nations of the earth. Aid to emerging nations is a necessary part of any stewardship of the nations of the world. The United States and other Western nations can share their wealth and technology in creative ways and develop policies that in a less personal way allow us Christian stewards to love our neighbors, even those on the other side of the planet Earth.

V
The Stewardship of Material Possessions

"For where your treasure is," Jesus teaches, "there will your heart be also" (Matt. 6:21). A person's relationship to the world of material things is a primary test of life's stewardship before God. In a strange way, money and the possessions it buys are an extension of the self, representing time, work, investment, achievement. Because of that intimate connection, one's attitude toward and relationship to material things is a particularly revealing test of his true priorities, sense of values, dominating concerns, and ultimate commitments.

A popular superficial viewpoint restricts the stewardship of material possessions primarily to the matter of giving generously to the causes of the kingdom of God and has little else to say about Christian economics. But one could give lavishly to the church and yet be a poor steward because of being a worshiper of mammon or because of squandering wealth on personal luxuries. The stewardship of material resources does involve giving but also one's attitude toward material things and practical total relationship to material things.

The Bible provides important principles about the stewardship of material possessions. This chapter will summarize many of those principles as a way of pointing toward a proper understanding of the place of material things in life and a responsible relationship to material things.

The Nature of Material Things

Human beings are creatures of the earth, with creaturely needs to be met and a dominion to be exercised. Man's divinely given dominion over the earth involves management, work, production, and subduing the earth. The Bible realistically assumes that property and accumulated wealth are integral to that role. How then are we to understand the nature of material things? The biblical principles help to define the legitimacy, purpose, dangers, and limits of material things.

The Legitimacy of Material Things

The Christian faith affirms the legitimacy of material things. The teachings of Jesus about material wealth and possessions appear somewhat contradictory on the surface. He admonishes his followers not to lay up earthly treasures for themselves, and yet he readily recognizes the validity of earthly needs and claims. For example, Jesus and his twelve apostles had a treasurer who kept their funds (see John 13:29). So alongside his warnings, he recognizes the legitimacy of wealth. Consequently, Jesus' occasional radical calls for people to abandon their property (e.g., Mark 10:21) are not universal demands for all followers but probably reflect his specific challenge to the worshipers of material wealth to shift their ultimate commitment to the kingdom of God.

The New Testament recognition of the legitimacy of material things grows out of the this-worldly, life-centered character of Hebrew religion. The Hebrews celebrated the good things—the sheer materiality—of the world. They regarded all wealth of the nation or of individuals, whether great or small, as a gift of God. Their understanding of the promise of God to Abraham involved the gift of the Promised Land, with its agricultural and mineral resources. Israel built into its yearly religious festivals cultic reminders that all the good things they enjoyed were not the result of nature's

71

kindness nor were they the result of their own hard work. All their material wealth was the gift of God and therefore required them to be obedient to God and to use their wealth to God's glory (see Deut. 4:1; 8:7 ff.; 8:17).

The New Testament also affirms the value of the material world, despite its frank recognition of the presence of radical evil in the world and of man's sinful preoccupation with the things of the world. In light of his redemption in Christ, the Christian is set free in relation to the world to enjoy its value without being dominated by its fallen power. In a pivotal passage, Paul says to Christians, "For *all things* are yours, whether Paul or Apollos or Cephas or the world or life or death or the present or the future, all are yours; and you are Christ's; and Christ is God's" (I Cor. 3:21-23; emphasis added).

The Dangers of Material Wealth

Although the New Testament recognizes the legitimacy of material things, it also repeatedly warns of the dangers attached to wealth and material possessions. Jesus requires that his followers live with a proper sense of priorities in relation to the absolute claim of the kingdom of God and that they pursue the things in life that have lasting value. Jesus did know that the affections of one's heart lie with the treasure it values most. Wealth, or the desire for it, has a way of dominating one's life. And it has adverse impact upon one's internal attitude, public life-style, and relationships within the church.

When material possessions take priority in life, that prevailing concern unleashes a variety of problems and sins, including anxiety, the abandonment of daily trust in God, covetousness, pride, and presumption. When people become preoccupied with making a living or accumulating wealth, they often fall into the grip of anxiety and discontentment and continually worry about what they will have tomorrow (see Matt. 6:25-34). Out of anxiety, one is then tempted to abandon one's daily trust in the providence of God and to take one's economic future into one's own hands. The desire for wealth also makes one covetous for what someone else has, a sin the Bible often warns against (see Exod. 20:17; Col. 3:5-6; et al.).

Wealth easily gives birth to social and economic pride. Paul warns the rich not to be haughty and flaunt their wealth over those of modest income or the poor (see I Tim. 6:17). Jesus told memorable stories about the rich who lord it over or ignore the poor. People who make wealth their high priority easily assume that wealth is evidence of the divine blessing and that poverty is a curse—a view not unknown in Hebrew history. The New Testament rejects completely any connection between wealth and divine blessing or between poverty and divine judgment. Such an attitude leads one to presume upon God and ignore the high demands of his Kingdom.

Wealth also poses severe dangers to one's style of life. Jesus says, "It is easier for a camel to go through the eye of a needle than for a rich man to enter the kingdom of God" (Mark 10:25). The problem occurs when one fails to understand that the kingdom of God must be central in one's life. Then the pursuit of wealth can become a dominating force. But Jesus asks, "For what does it profit a man, to gain the whole world and forfeit his life?" (Mark 8:36). Man must choose between living for God and living for the accumulation of wealth. "No one can serve two masters. . . . You cannot serve God and mammon" (Matt. 6:24).

Wealth continues to represent a peril for many people who have entered the Kingdom by faith and have become members of the church. Christians with above-average wealth can easily posture within the congregation and claim power commensurate with their economic status. As in the apostolic church, they can create an appearance of generosity while in fact being stingy with their resources (see, e.g., Acts 4). Wealth can even break the bond of fellowship within the church. James points out how poorer members of the church can be excessively deferential to the rich in the congregation who are their very own economic repressors (see James

2:1-7). Paul suggests that "the love of money is the root of all evils," leading men into temptation, ruin, and destruction. It even causes some to wander away from the faith (see I Tim. 6:8-10).

The Limitations of Wealth

The New Testament recognizes the legitimacy of material resources within the overall stewardship of life, as long as one maintains proper priorities. As Jesus observed, "A man's life does not consist in the abundance of his possessions" (Luke 12:15). If a person makes wealth his highest priority and ultimate value, he will come up empty-handed at some critical points in life. Money cannot buy much of life's most important values. It cannot buy the gift of new life nor can it buy the gifts of the Spirit (see Acts 8:18-24; I Pet. 1:18-19). It provides no help in distress nor in the hour of death (see Job 36:19). So Jesus advises, "Do not lay up for yourselves treasures on earth, . . . but lay up for yourselves treasures in heaven" (Matt. 6:19-21).

The power of wealth is limited by the two awesome realities of physical death and final judgment. Paul reminds us that "we brought nothing into the world, and we cannot take anything out of the world" (I Tim. 6:7). Job recognized that money cannot buy God's favor in the judgment (see Job 34:19). Jesus stresses that the judgment is unexpected. His warning to the rich man is, "Fool! This night your soul is required of you; and the things you have prepared, whose will they be?" (Luke 12:20). The judgment will terminate man's relationship to his possessions (see Matt. 24:37 ff.).

The Steward and His Possessions

The Christian stewardship of material resources requires more than an understanding of material things in the divine purposes and a right attitude about the material world. A right attitude must be translated into one's actual relationship to material things in the acquisition, use, and final disposition of wealth.

The Acquisition of Wealth

Various biblical principles provide guidance about how the Christian is to acquire his wealth. A right attitude should underlie any effort to earn income or to accumulate material wealth. When one trusts God to provide for basic material needs, one is freed from anxiety about tomorrow (see Matt. 6:25-34). Such trust is possible only when a person seeks first the kingdom of God and then orders priorities in relation to that ultimate commitment.

Another recurrent biblical principle is that all able-bodied persons are to earn their income by honest work if possible. Paul, for example, condemned idle people in the Thessalonian church who were living off the labor of others. He exhorted them "to do their work in quietness and to earn their own living" (II Thess. 3:12). The earning of income in modern societies is far more complicated than it was in the first century, particularly in capitalist economies based upon investment, productivity, and profit. But the principle can apply to any work that represents energy, investment, creativity, and a constructive contribution to society.

A third principle is that wealth must not be gained at the expense of others. Early Hebrew laws prohibited making a profit off a poor brother (see Lev. 25:35 ff.) or charging interest on loans to the poor (see Exod. 22:25). Because of widespread disregard of these laws, the prophets thundered out condemation of those who gained wealth at the expense of the poor (see Amos 2:6-7; 5:10-12; Mic. 2:12; et al.). The prophets even foresaw the nation's being destroyed because of massive injustice to the poor (see Isa. 11:3-5). The New Testament also condemns the acquisition of wealth at the expense of others. Jesus identified heavily with the poor. He condemned the Pharisees who devour widows' houses (see Luke 20:47) and the rich who live sumptuously while ignoring the poor (see Luke 16:19-31). He denounced the money changers in the temple who profited from the worshipers' temple contributions (see Matt. 21:12). James scathingly condemned the idle rich who defraud their field workers (see James 5:1-4).

A fourth principle is the necessity of integrity and honesty in labor and employment. Hebrew laws required the use of honest weights and measures in business transactions (see Deut. 25:13-14). The Ephesians writer even dares to use the relationship of a master and a slave to illustrate the importance of honest work and honest compensation in economic relationships (see Eph. 6:5-9). There are powerful implications in this principle for Christian vocation and for labor-management relationships in society.

Finally, the acquisition of wealth must not be allowed to dominate one's life so that the pursuit of possessions becomes an end in itself. The psalmist noted that the ultimate danger is that "the man greedy for gain curses and renounces the Lord" (Ps. 10:3). Or Jesus observes that only the fool lays up treasure for himself and is not rich toward God (see Luke 12:21). To those dominated by the quest for material wealth, Jesus asks, "For what does it profit a man, to gain the whole world and forfeit his life?" (Mark 8:36).

What about ownership of property or goods? The view that God is the owner of all creation extends specifically to his ultimate ownership of all created things and of all individual possessions. Therefore God sets the limits for human ownership, both individual and collective. Biblical thought stresses our common ownership of the planet's resources. It teaches that the world's natural resources must be preserved for posterity and must not be controlled by a few people. This collective dimension of ownership determined Israel's regulations about the use of the land in Palestine. They believed that God himself gave them the Promised Land and that the gift carried with it attendant responsibilities in its use. They regarded God as owner and themselves as temporary tenants and stewards of the land. Recognizing that they did not have unlimited use of the land, the Hebrews developed numerous regulations about the use of the land, agricultural methods, policies for feeding the poor and travelers with the land's produce, and buying and selling the land. The different tithes reminded them of their temporary occupancy (see Lev. 27:30-32; Deut. 14:22-27; Num. 18:31-32).

The Hebrews valued and respected both communal and private property within Israel. During the nomadic period, pastures and water were common tribal property. When agriculture developed within Israel, arable land was occasionally held in common, particularly in the early period (see Num. 26:55-56; 33:54; et al.). Family property was also important. Family identity was often tied up with property, which frequently contained the family ancestral tombs (see Josh. 24:30; I Sam. 25:1). It was unlawful to remove boundary markers (see Deut. 19:24). Extensive inheritance laws were designed to keep family property within the family (see Num. 27:7-11; Deut. 25:5-10; Lev. 25:25).

The New Testament also accepts the legitimacy of property. Jesus apparently approved of private property and sound investment. He used the idea of property and productive investment as the parabolic setting for important teachings about the kingdom of God (see, e.g., Luke 19:11 ff.). At the same time, the New Testament accentuates the temporary nature of human ownership. Jesus indicates that no matter how much wealth one accumulates, death strips it all away (see Luke 12:13-21). Material wealth is strictly an earthly phenomenon.

The Use of Material Possessions

How should a good steward use his material wealth and possessions? The key principle is: In responsible freedom in accordance with the divine purposes in creation and redemption. The purposes of material wealth within the overall purposes of God relate to the individual and to his relationship with others. In relation to the self, material possessions represent God's gift of the basic necessities of life—food, clothing, and housing (see Matt. 6:25-33; I Tim.

6:8-9). God gives us all good things to enjoy but not to turn into ends in themselves (see I Tim. 6:17). As a gift, our possessions are a potential instrument of creative expression, one element in our mandate to exercise dominion in the earth. Our use of material possessions is a major test of the quality of our stewardship. The explosive possibilities in our modern scientific-technological economy, particularly, need to be shaped by the biblical imperative to utilize our resources for the good of the whole human family.

The purposes of material wealth also relate to our lives within society. Our wealth should be used to care for our family, as both Jesus and Paul taught (see Matt. 15:3-6; I Tim. 5:8, 16). The Christian also should support government services through taxation. Jesus taught that Jewish citizens should pay taxes to Caesar (see Matt. 22:15-21; cf. Rom. 13:1). The Christian should use his wealth to care for the needy—the hungry, thirsty, sick, imprisoned, homeless, widowed, orphaned, and poor (see, e.g., James 2:15-16; Matt. 24:31-46; et al.). Paul says that the financially rich "are to do good, to be rich in good deeds, liberal and generous" (I Tim. 6:18). Finally, the Christian is to use his wealth in support of the gospel—in such things as supporting ministers (see I Cor. 9:14; I Tim. 5:5-17) and giving to the church on a regular basis (see I Cor. 16:2). To sum up, the Christian can justify using his material resources for any purpose that cares for basic human needs or enriches and ennobles human life through the pursuit of truth, the creation of beauty, or the struggle for human rights, justice, and dignity.

A Christian style of life should become the key determinant of the particular ways in which the Christian uses his material resources, and that style should reflect one's wholehearted commitment to the kingdom of God. Because God provides our material resources, the Christian should be content with what is his. That is a healthy antidote to a consumer-oriented, Madison Avenue–afflicted society. Paul suggests, "There is great gain in godliness with contentment; . . . but if we have food and clothing, with these we shall be content" (I Tim. 6:6-8).

Sacrificial living is a second dimension of a Christian life-style. Jesus calls his followers to sacrifice in the service of the kingdom of God (see Mark 10:28-31). What is *sacrifice*? It is hard to define and is perhaps relative from one society to another. *Sacrifice* might be simply defined as that kind of life that is lived at a simpler and less acquisitional level than that lived by people in similar vocations and social settings.

A Christian life-style also distinguishes between needs and luxuries. Like sacrifice, luxuries may be relative from one person to another. A stereo system might represent an incidental luxury to a non–music lover. But to a student or lover of music a stereo might represent an aesthetic need that enriches and fulfills that particular individual. What cannot be reconciled with Christian commitment is a life that wallows in excessive luxury or that is consumed with a desire to attain that level of luxury. The same principle might apply to expensive, frivolous possessions. Many luxuries ought rightly to be sacrificed to the cause of the kingdom of God.

Sound management of one's economic resources is another characteristic of an informed Christian life-style. Parables like that of the pounds (see Luke 19:11-27) or the talents (see Matt. 25:14-30) have various implications that grow out of their central point. There is a clear principle related to the kingdom of God: We are to invest our resources in life in order to multiply them for the sake of the Kingdom. That idea covers all of life, not primarily material wealth. But when one applies the principle to economics, as one part of life's resources, its meaning will vary with the kind of economic system under which one lives. In the United States where modified capitalism prevails, investment and credit are basic to the functioning of the system. How one manages and invests will vary with the financial resources of different families and individuals. For some it might mean major investment in the stock market, bonds, income property, and business enterprises. Good stewardship demands careful calculations and investments.

But for many average families, sound management might have more to do with a family budget, with buying a house, cars, furniture, appliances, clothing, groceries, and recreational items. And here, in the most common way, good stewardship requires basic business skills that allow us to use most effectively our financial resources for our maximum benefit. A good Christian should not squander his money or carelessly invest it.

Material resources should also be used to ensure a dignified future for oneself and one's family. Here the Christian steward's responsibilities are bound up with existing programs and policies in his society. A basic dimension of stewardship is the purchase of adequate insurance to care for a family or spouse in case of the steward's death or a disabling injury. Support of the Social Security system is one aspect of intelligent Christian stewardship. In our era of rapid inflation, most people need additional programs that provide retirement security. There are various kinds of retirement and annuity programs. Most major corporations, businesses, and institutions have substantial provisions and programs to assure the future security of their employees. Many people can utilize tax-sheltered programs during the maximum income-earning years for increased retirement investment. In addition, many people have the financial resources to invest in property, stocks and bonds, and other income-producing enterprises. With the lengthened life expectancy of today's Americans, retirement stewardship has become critically important.

The Disposition of Material Resources

The New Testament observes, "For we brought nothing into the world, and we cannot take anything out of the world" (I Tim. 6:7). Most people, whether wealthy or poor, leave some treasure behind. The treasure might be cash, property, investments, stocks and bonds, a bank account, insurance, household furniture, or other valuables. The responsible steward should deliberately determine that his estate, whatever its value, should go to productive uses that reflect his own priorities. What those uses are will vary among particular individuals. Most people want to, and usually should, provide for their families. Many wish to leave some wealth to a church institution or other major human causes. Depending upon one's view of what is important in life, those causes might include scientific research, medical research, education, cultural enterprises, social services, ecological concerns, and many other, broader human concerns. Here we must respect the freedom and responsibility of the individual Christian to make his own value judgments. Good stewardship does, however, require that the final disposition of wealth be determined by one's primary commitment to the kingdom of God and to the value and dignity of the human family.

The responsible steward should develop an estate plan that allows him to control his own estate and avoid having an arbitrary estate plan imposed by law if he should die without a will or other disposition arrangements. The plan should effectively pass on property and other financial holdings to his family and other beneficiaries as well as provide financial security during possible disability or retirement. It should be devised to pass on maximum wealth to beneficiaries with a minimum of loss through inflation, taxation, probate and transfer costs, and the uncertainty of court litigation at death.

An individual may dispose of his estate in various ways during his lifetime, at death, or at the death of his primary family survivors or other beneficiaries. A comprehensive plan will provide for the disposition of all tangible and intangible properties through such methods as the will, insurance, cash gifts, various types of trust, and other means. Because of the complexity of laws relating to the passing of estates and occasional changes in tax laws, an individual would be wise to develop his estate plan in consultation with professional estate consultants.

Although certain parts of an estate—such as insurance, trusts, or jointly held property or stocks—may at death pass outside a will, the *will* is a critical part of an overall estate plan. Through a will the individual determines how, when, and to whom his property will be distributed. It allows him, not a court, to name the executor of his estate and the guardian of his young children and their inherited property. The will can create trusts for a spouse, children, or other beneficiaries who may not be competent in money management. One can also make several types of tax-free charitable gifts through his will. A carefully drawn will may reduce, and in some cases eliminate, taxes. As a general rule, the will should be drawn by a competent lawyer.

One should also be alert to the possibilities of passing wealth to charitable institutions at death outside of a will. *Life insurance policies*, for example, allow an individual to designate as beneficiary an institution or church agency or to designate an institution as the contingent beneficiary when the primary beneficiary is no longer living. In a similar way, *trusts* that were established during one's lifetime may be designed to pass automatically to designated institutions at death.

As important as the will is in the orderly final disposition of an estate, there are other methods of disposing of wealth that effectively pass on property to the family and others, provide income security during retirement and disability, and minimize income, gift, estate, and inheritance taxes. For example, one may save estate taxes by making *cash gifts* within legal limits to family members and others during one's lifetime. *Outright gifts* of cash, property, stocks and bonds, or other assets to charitable institutions also save both estate and income taxes. Such gifts are particularly useful for people who have adequate retirement security. Outright gifts may take several forms. The donor may allow the institution to use the principle of the gift or restrict it to use of income from the endowment investment of the principle. The donor also may designate how his gift must be used, or he may consign that choice to the institution.

Retained life income trusts provide another useful way of giving to important causes while at the same time ensuring income for one's own lifetime or that of a primary survivor. There are basically two types of life income trusts. The *revocable charitable remainder trust,* which provides maximum flexibility for the donor, is created when an individual places most of his assets in trust and then receives the income. He can withdraw all or part of the principle or revoke the provisions of the trust before his death. But unless revoked, the trust passes at his death to the designated institution or beneficiary according to the terms of the trust.

A second type of trust is the *irrevocable charitable remainder trust,* which may take the form of either an annuity trust or a unitrust. In the irrevocable trust, the donor transfers cash or other securities to a trustee who invests and manages the trust and pays the donor income for life, according to the terms of the trust. At the death of the donor or his designated primary survivor, the trust becomes the sole property of the charitable institution. In general, there are higher tax benefits during one's lifetime for outright gifts or for irrevocable charity remainder trusts.

Most major Christian churches and denominations have now established foundations that assist Christians in making decisions about the final disposition of their wealth and estates. Stewardship education in individual congregations should inform Christians of available services and challenge them to responsible final disposition of their material resources. It does matter how we acquire, use, and dispose of the wealth that God makes available to us.

VI
The Art of Giving

In the only recorded words of Jesus outside the Gospels, he said, "It is more blessed to give than to receive" (Acts 20:35). Giving is an art, and God is the master teacher. Giving is a pattern at the very heart of reality itself, written there in creation and redemption. The universe, human existence, and redemption are all gifts from God. The greatest gift of all and the model for Christian giving is God's gift of his Son. Paul appeals to that model in his most important passage on giving, in which he urges early Christians to give to the Jerusalem relief offering. At the end of it he breaks into praise, "Thanks be to God for his inexpressible gift!" (II Cor. 9:15). It should be no surprise that giving is at the very heart of Christian stewardship.

Modern stewardship movements have grasped and stressed the importance of giving. Unfortunately, however, the deeper theological dimensions of stewardship do not always accompany prevailing practices. Unworthy approaches to giving can easily slip innocently unawares into popular stewardship programs. Some churches can be trapped by the temptation to wrench the stewardship of giving out of the larger context of the stewardship of life and then to make giving the singular focus of stewardship. Perhaps nowhere else in the life of some churches is legalism a more alluring temptation. In few other places can institutional values more easily be substituted for concern for the growth of persons into spiritual maturity.

It is imperative that the church follow a sound approach in developing a theology and practice of the stewardship of giving. The Bible is the obvious starting point for most churches and Christians. It provides the clues and guiding principles for whatever we do in the life of faith. Regrettably, some stewardship literature and practices have utilized too much careless, indiscriminate, and uninformed interpretation of the Bible in the stewardship of giving. For one thing, New Testament teachings are easily bypassed for Old Testament practices. But in responsible biblical interpretation, Old Testament teachings and practices must always be weighed and evaluated by how they are taken up, transformed, and sometimes transcended or set aside by New Testament teachings and practices. The result is that some stewardship teachings much more resemble Hebrew law than Christian grace and more resemble Old Testament rules than New Testament principles. When that happens, the freedom and responsibility of the individual Christian is set aside for the authority of the church's detailed formulation of what Christian giving entails.

When the church develops a program of giving, that program should reflect the Christian faith's central commitment to the responsible freedom of the individual. Giving too, as all of life, should be related to the divine process of person-making. And the individual in turn should seek the clearest and most definitive guidelines in Scripture and theology for his stewardship of giving. So, how do we understand giving? What are its scope and purpose? What are appropriate motivational principles and giving procedures?

The Scope and Purpose of Giving

Christian giving originates in the gifts of God in creation and redemption. The Christian can give nothing that he has not first received from God. All giving originates in the divine love that wills to share himself with his creatures. Giving is therefore the natural response of creatures made in the image of God, particularly as they are being transformed into the fullness of that image through faith in Jesus Christ. Giving is the normal expression of grateful faith, a recognition of the costly nature of grace and the radical demands of Christian discipleship.

The Scope of Giving

Within the overall stewardship of life, the Christian is commanded to give a portion of all his personal and material resources to serve God and man. Generous giving is not a substitute for the adequate total stewardship of life. But on the other hand, one cannot be a good steward of one's total resources without developing and practicing the art of generous giving. Far too often, giving is focused solely upon money. It is important to give generously of one's financial wealth. But the stewardship of giving also encompasses the giving of ourselves, our time, and our abilities in the service of God and man. There are Christians who are generous with their finances but who let large material gifts become a substitute for the sharing of the other personal, nonmaterial wealth that God has given us. Responsible church membership requires the Christian to give generously of his time and abilities in the service of the kingdom of God. The principle of proportionate giving applies to these treasures quite as much as to one's bank account.

Yet, at the same time, it is true that among life's resources money has an unusual potential for good or evil. Because in a sense money represents an extension of the self, financial giving is a particularly good barometer for indicating how generous and loving the Christian steward actually is. The wealth for which the Christian steward is accountable in giving includes all income and accumulated wealth. The Christian is not given the luxury of selective accountability. In a capitalist economy, our income and wealth can come from a variety of sources. Good stewardship requires that all wealth, from whatever source, be included as the treasure for our proportionate giving. Those sources include salary, interest, capital gain, bonuses, rent, payments, royalties, honoraria, bequests, inheritance, judgments, rewards, and various other sources.

The Christian should develop his practices in giving from whatever clear directives and helpful principles he can gain from the New Testament. Yet in the final analysis only the individual steward himself can determine when, where, what, and how he will give. As with his total stewardship, the Christian steward will determine his giving in responsible freedom. That is the freedom of grace. Christ has set the Christian free from the letter of the Old Testament law, including laws of tithes and offerings. Christian freedom, however, is not lawlessness. Responsible is the necessary qualifier. The Christian lives in *responsible* freedom. He is bound by his service to Christ and by the demands of love. Therefore he will seek the best biblical guidance about God's expectations for the giving of his servants. But there are complex situations where there are no clear guidelines. So the giver himself must be responsible for the use and giving of his financial resources. But we remain accountable for our generosity or lack of it in giving. It is a principle of life that "he who sows sparingly will also reap sparingly," says Paul, "and he who sows bountifully will also reap bountifully" (II Cor. 9:6).

The Purpose of Giving

What is the purpose of giving? Paul provides a brief inclusive insight into the purpose of giving in a comment to the Corinthians about their share in the Jerusalem offering. "Under the test of this service," he writes, "you will glorify God by your obedience in acknowledging the gospel of Christ, and by the generosity of your contribution for them and for all others" (II Cor. 9:13). Here he indicates three purposes in giving, and he intimates a fourth. The purposes are (1) to glorify God, (2) to serve the needs of man, (3) to discipline and mature the self in the venture of faith, and (4) to support the life, ministry, and mission of the church (implied in acknowledging the gospel of Christ).

87

The first purpose of giving is to glorify God. Giving is an expression of praise and thanksgiving. It acknowledges that God is sovereign in the universe and is the source of all of life's blessings. The Hebrew tithes and offerings were designed in part to teach people to fear and honor God (see Deut. 14:34). Paul describes the Jerusalem offering as overflowing in many thanksgivings to God (see II Cor. 9:12).

The second purpose of giving is to serve the needs of man. Our love of God is inseparably tied to our love of man. A major way of expressing our love to God is to love man. In the Hebrew tithing system, the Hebrews gave part of their tithes and various charity gifts to serve directly the needs of people (see Deut. 14:28-29). The New Testament indicates that one major purpose of giving is to alleviate different forms of human need and problems. This dimension is so important that Jesus teaches that when we give to people in need, we give directly to the Lord himself (see Matt. 25:31-46).

A third purpose of giving is to discipline the self in growth toward higher levels of maturity in the Christian life. The great commandment requires not only that we love God but that we love our neighbors as ourselves (see Luke 10:27). A goal of the Christian life is to break out of the bonds of self-interest. Giving is a revealing test of how far we have traveled toward that goal. Giving is love in action. Giving is an exercise in opening our grasping, possessive hands and extending love to another. It is a clue as to whether we are laying up treasures in heaven or are in the business of building bigger barns. One's ease in giving is an accurate barometer of one's sense of value and degree of loving generosity.

A fourth purpose of giving is to support the life, ministry, and mission of the church. When one is baptized into the church, one is incorporated into the full range of the church's existence and service of the gospel. Financial support is basic to the church's internal life and external mission and ministry. Financial support is one aspect of what Paul refers to as partnership in the gospel (see Phil. 4:15). Generous giving undergirds the church's work in the world. In supporting a wide range of ministries, services, and personnel, giving allows one indirectly to go, serve, and love where physically one may never be able to go. And through the church's work, the gospel is preached and people are served to the glory of God.

Motivation in and Procedures for Giving

Jesus stresses the importance of the inward intention as well as of the outward act. The value of a good action can be nullified or weakened by unworthy motivation or procedures. Jesus sharply rebukes some people who give for the wrong reasons or in the wrong way. Each individual alone can know his own intention in giving, although his manner of giving may be very public. The church should design proper motivational principles and procedures into its approach to giving. Helpful insights are found throughout the Bible. The teachings of Jesus and of Paul are especially useful for providing motivational principles and procedures. Paul's major passages on giving to the Jerusalem offering, in I Corinthians 16:1-4 and II Corinthians 8 and 9, provide an outstanding example of creative leadership motivating Christians to give.

Motivation for Giving

Modern stewardship programs have not infrequently embodied unworthy motivational appeals. Many church members can give for unworthy motives. Christian stewardship should be alert to many unacceptables motives. One should not give, for example, in order to gain acclaim and recognition. Jesus specifically warns against giving so as to be seen by men (see Matt. 6:1). One should not give in order to receive a reward or to prosper. Jesus says the giver should expect nothing in return for his gift (see Luke 6:32-36). One should not give in order to manipulate God or try to gain his favor. Giving is simply the duty of the servant of God (see Luke 17:7-10).

In the contemporary setting, there are other unworthy motives for giving. Some people give in order to gain power over a group. Some give in an effort to satisfy the demands of conscience but do so reluctantly and complainingly. Many people give out a sense of pressure from manipulative stewardship campaigns by their churches. In those cases, the church may get their money, but God has not really gotten their heart and deepest allegiances. There are people who give in calculated public displays of generosity, in ways designed to enhance their business or political possibilities or esteem in the community's eye. There are people who give primarily for the purpose of getting maximum mileage out of their tax deductions and write-offs, and little more.

The value of Christian giving depends heavily upon one's motives. The church should educate members about proper motivations in giving and should utilize only distinctive Christian motivations in the financial programs of the church. In the long run, the church will not only receive more gifts for important ministries but will facilitate the spiritual growth of church members if it abandons Madison Avenue for biblical principles of motivation. The following are important biblical motivational principles stated in terms that can easily be translated into the financial programs of the average church.

1. *Give as a response to God's grace.* Paul calls giving a "gracious work" (II Cor. 8:7). The Christian has nothing he has not first received from God (see I Cor. 4:7). Both the act of giving and the material gift we give are gifts we ourselves have received as beneficiaries of God's goodness. The Christian can rise to the Christian standard of giving only as God's saving grace frees us to give as God has given to us (see II Cor. 9:8). Christian giving depends upon God's grace toward us and upon grace at work within us.

2. *Give as a response to the example of Christ who gave himself for us.* God's gift of Christ is the prototype of all giving. "For you

know the grace of our Lord Jesus Christ," comments Paul, "that though he was rich, yet for your sake he became poor, so that by his poverty you might become rich" (II Cor. 8:9).

3. *Give as a response to human need.* This principle is as old as the early chapters of Hebrew history. The good Samaritan most memorably embodies the principle (see Luke 10:29-37). Paul suggests that the believer out of his own abundance should supply the needy person's wants (see II Cor. 8:14).

4. *Give as an expression of thanksgiving to God.* Giving is an integral part of worship. Although its origins are lost in antiquity, giving was formalized in various ways in Hebrew religion, the thank offering being a prime example (see Lev. 7:12-13). Paul even speaks of the Jerusalem offering for the famine-stricken saints as overflowing in many thanksgivings to God (see II Cor. 9:12).

5. *Give as a form of sacrifice to God.* From the earliest stages of Hebrew religion, gifts have been basic to the sacrificial system. Even in the New Testament, gifts given directly to other human beings in need can be described as sacrifices to God. In daring language, Paul calls the Philippians' gift to himself "a fragrant offering, a sacrifice acceptable and pleasing to God" (Phil. 4:18).

6. *Give as a way of symbolizing one's commitment of all one's resources to the service of God and man.* This principle is found, to one degree or another, in all biblical giving practices. God is consistently viewed as owner of everything, even in practices that view the tithes, firstfruits, and firstborn as belonging peculiarly to God (see Exod. 22:28-29; 23:19). But in the New Testament it is central that "you are not your own; you were bought with a price" (I Cor. 6:20). God has absolute claim upon all that we are and have. Therefore our acts of giving should become a symbolic commitment of all our other financial resources to the purposes of God.

7. *Give as a concrete proof of love.* Love is not good intention or warm emotion. It is acting, reaching out, translating words into acts. According to Paul, the gift of the Gentile churches

91

to the needy Jerusalem church was proof of genuine love (see II Cor. 8:8, 24).

Procedures in Giving

It is important *how* we give. Procedures and methods in giving will vary with the objects of concern to which one gives. Yet despite differences of detailed application, certain principles are found throughout the Bible that should inform how we give in a variety of situations.

1. *Put first things first.* A person's basic commitment in life is more important than any particular gift. When the steward obeys Jesus' command to seek first the kingdom of God (see Matt. 6:33), everything else will fall into its proper place, including responsible giving.

2. *Give the self before any material gift.* It is always tempting to substitute a material gift for the giving of oneself to God or to a person in need. The Old Testament prophets repeatedly condemned this practice. The giver should identify himself with his gift. Paul notes that before the Macedonian Christians contributed to the Jerusalem offering, "first they gave themselves to the Lord and to us" (II Cor. 8:5).

3. *Give God the first and best that we possess.* The Old Testament system of giving required that the firstfruits of the harvest and the best offspring of the animals be for God (see Exod. 22:29 f.; Deut. 17:1; Mal. 1:6 f.). In giving God first claim to our income and possessions, the steward symbolically dedicates the remainder of his resources to God.

4. *Give voluntarily.* The only gift that honors God is one that comes freely from a willing, loving heart. Jesus insisted that the response to God must transcend the legal obligation of Hebrew religion, involving the intention as well as the outward act. Paul applied that principle in his effort to collect funds for the Jerusalem church. He insisted that giving must not be an exaction from a reluctant spirit but only an expression of one's own free will (see II Cor. 8:3; 9:5). One of Paul's inviolable principles for giving is this: "Each one must do as he has made up his mind, not reluctantly or under

compulsion, for God loves a cheerful giver" (II Cor. 9:7).

5. *Give proportionately as God prospers.* Proportionate giving is the basis for the Old Testament tithing system and the key principle for the New Testament approach to giving. In removing giving from a legal basis, the New Testament retains the idea of the individual's giving as God has prospered him. But here proportionate giving is more dynamic and flexible than in the Old Testament. Other dimensions must help determine what proportion of one's income represents a loving commitment to the kingdom of God, particularly at the lower and upper ends of the financial-wealth spectrum (see I Cor. 16:2). Paul observes, "It is acceptable according to what a man has, not according to what he has not" (II Cor. 8:12).

6. *Give generously.* In the New Testament, the liberality of love supercedes Old Testament legalism. Generosity becomes the guiding principle, not percentage rules. Paul notes that the generous Corinthian gift to Jerusalem overflows in a wealth of liberality (see II Cor. 8:2; 9:11).

7. *Give sacrificially.* Jesus made hard demands upon his followers. Many of his parables are directed toward the peril of riches and the need for radical sacrifice. His estimate of the generosity of any material gift is measured not by the size of the gift but by how much is left over after the gift is made. He lavishly commended the widow for the amount of sacrificial love represented by her small but total gift. In comparison with the rich, Jesus said, "this poor widow has put in more than all of them; for they all contributed out of their abundance, but she out of her poverty put in all the living that she had" (Luke 21:3-4).

8. *Give spontaneously.* Giving cannot be restricted to the channel of the institutional church. Many immediate face-to-face human needs demand a spontaneous personal response. Jesus strongly affirmed the importance of giving alms to the needy, a practice long hallowed by Jewish tradition (see Matt. 6:2-4). The Christian must serve the needs of the poor, hungry, homeless, and sick whenever and

wherever they are encountered (see Matt. 25:31-46). The modern church may have a tendency to minimize the importance of one-to-one caring in its stress upon giving to the church. No amount of church giving can offset the failure to give personal help as worthy needs arise.

9. *Give systematically.* Responsible giving requires planned and regular patterns that avoid spasmodic giving. The Old Testament tithing system built in regular procedures. In connection with the Jerusalem offering, Paul advised setting aside part of one's income on the first day of each week (see I Cor. 16:2). At a minimum, the Christian should ideally follow the practice of weekly giving, although other methods might be additionally necessary.

10. *Give humbly.* Jesus warned about performing acts of piety for public display. In particular, he taught that almsgiving should be done in secret (see Matt. 6:1-4). Although giving in the modern church cannot be done in the strictest privacy because of the need to keep tax records, among other things, the Christian should never make a show of his giving. If the contemporary church took this principle seriously, it would immediately alter a number of practices.

11. *Give in love.* Just as Christian giving loses its value without a prior commitment to the kingdom of God, so it misses its purpose if it is done without love. No form of giving can ever be substituted for love. Authentic giving is one expression of our growth into the kind of person God wants us to be. But mechanical giving is no guarantee that we have tapped the nature of love. Paul warns, "If I give away all I have, . . . but have not love, I gain nothing" (I Cor. 13:3).

Giving and Rewards

A prominent businessman once said: "The minute I started my partnership with God and began to tithe, my business boomed. And across the years, the sky has been the limit. You can't outgive God!" Similar testimonials are common-place in many church budget or financial campaigns. Many honest, sincere, conscientious Christians believe that Christian giving or tithing is a good business investment and will reap a financial reward.

What about rewards for Christian giving? There are two extreme views. One argues that the hope for a reward is a worthy motive for action in life or for Christian giving. On the opposite side is the view that any thought of a reward compromises a good deed. The New Testament teachings will satisfy neither extreme view.

Many people who anticipate a reward for their giving appeal to Old Testament passages for their authority. There are major traditions in Hebrew life that appealed to material rewards as a motive for good actions. Jesus, however, radically changed those traditional teachings on reward and rejected a materialist view. At the same time, rewards are basic to New Testament thought, but never as a proper *motive* for right actions. Rewards are always viewed as the gift of God, not as wages one has earned (see Matt. 20:1-16; Luke 17:7-10). The rewards are primarily spiritual, not material, and are related to the basic values of the kingdom of God, which reverse our fallen human values (see Luke 10:20; Matt. 5:3-12; II Cor. 4:17). They are for the most part to be conferred in the future judgment (Luke 14:12-14; Gal. 6:7 ff.; Rom. 6:21). However, there are also present rewards, such as enjoying the values of the Christian life and of fellowship within the Christian Church (see Matt. 19:29).

One thing is certain. The New Testament teachings do not promise economic rewards or riches for the giving of one's wealth. Jesus and his apostles advocated a radical new scale of values based upon the assertion that life does not consist in the abundance of things (see Matt. 6:19-21, 31-33; Luke 12:15; 19:21-22). The Christian is promised that God will provide for his basic material needs in life (see Matt. 6:33; II Cor. 9:8; Phil. 4:19). But there is no promise of affluence or riches. True personal worth depends upon God's loving acceptance of an individual in Christ, not upon the size of his bank account. To the contrary, far from promising his disciples economic affluence, Jesus calls us to a life of self-denial, sacrifice, and even potential suffering in the service of the Kingdom (see Luke 14:25-33).

Good financial stewards sometimes prosper economically. But, of course, so do many poor stewards and non-Christians as well. And some good Christian stewards may live at substandard or even bare survival levels. However, when Christian stewards do prosper, they should be grateful to God and use the overflow in service to God (see Phil. 3:7-10; II Cor. 11:1 ff.).

When does an act receive a reward from God? Jesus is quite clear that any act, if it is to be rewarded, must be done for the right motive, in the correct way, to those who need love and service and cannot return the good deed. If one aims at a reward in doing good, one will lose a reward (see Luke 6:32-36). If one serves or loves only those who can return a good deed, there will be no reward (see Luke 14:12-14). If one performs a good deed or generous act for the purpose of receiving public acclaim, then the acclaim itself is its own reward. The act will receive no further reward from God (see Matt. 6:1-8, 16-18).

With such qualifications on what kinds of acts will be rewarded, one can begin to understand why Jesus taught that some who will be rewarded at the Judgment will be surprised. Their serving of man is so selfless that they have not only not anticipated a reward, they are not even conscious of doing the kind of deeds that might be rewarded (see Matt. 25:31-46). God will reward good stewardship at any level in terms of the values of the kingdom of God, but only when the stewardship is lived within the guidelines set by Jesus.

VII
Concerns in Giving

Christian giving, as all of stewardship, should be related to the divine purposes in creation and redemption. Consequently, the concerns in giving are as broad as life itself. Giving is more than an ecclesiastical affair. And there is part of the problem. Hundreds of worthy causes bid for the Christian's financial support. With limited resources, one cannot give to everything. The practical difficulty is how to establish priorities in giving. How do we determine where, how, and how much to give of our financial resources in order to best serve God's purposes in the world?

In the broadest sense, the Christian glorifies God by giving to serve the needs of man and to support the life, ministry, and mission of the church. But there are myriads of human needs. The Bible does provide some broad guidelines for giving to these areas of concern. But it cannot answer specific questions or resolve precisely how we should balance our giving to the church and to causes outside the church.

The problem is complicated by the fact that the biblical pattern of giving was developed in a theocratic culture where there was no clear distinction between the responsibilities of the state and the responsibilities of the religious institutions. And now in the modern era the state and secular agencies have assumed responsibility for many human concerns that were traditionally often cared for through ministries of the church, such as welfare, care of the aged, medical care, and education. Now the Christian supports many of these human services through taxation or charitable gifts. The only adequate procedure today is for the individual steward to exercise responsibility for his own giving within the best possible biblical-theological guidelines and his personal sense of commitment.

Giving to the Church

Although Christian giving is more extensive than giving to the church, a committed Christian will give a substantial portion of his proportionate giving to the church. If the steward gives according to the will of God as revealed in Jesus Christ, he will share in the life and work of the church.

Giving Within the Family of God

Why should the individual steward give substantially to the church? Perhaps it would be enough to say that we stand under the divine command that is rooted in the tithing traditions of the Old Testament. From the earliest era of Hebrew life, the Hebrew covenant with God included the regular giving of tithes and offerings to support the priesthood and religious cultus, the local sanctuaries, and finally the Jerusalm temple (see Num. 18:21 ff.; et al.). Their giving expressed love, adoration, thanksgiving, and commitment to the God of the covenant. Because the church is so central in the purposes of God, it surely deserves no less (see Eph. 1:22; 3:10).

But a legalistic command is not the best way to facilitate the growth of persons into spiritual maturity. There is a better approach that will encourage the Christian to experience the joy of generous giving to the church while he exercises his own personal freedom and responsibility. The key is the idea of the church as covenant community. Among the various ways the New Testament expresses this corporate nature of the church is the powerful image of Christians as "members of the household of God" (Eph. 2:19).

Stewardship is a family affair! We are redeemed into the

church, the family of God (see Eph. 2:16). When the Christian joins the church, he becomes a member of a new spiritual family that places a claim upon his life and resources. Within that family relationship, the steward abandons his autonomy and uses his freedom and responsibility in relation to the common commitments of the church. While the church must respect the freedom and responsibility of the individual, the responsible steward will freely support the life and work of the church.

Much of God's work in the world is accomplished through the life, ministry, and mission of the church. Christians assume mutual responsibility for that. Christian stewards share their lives, time, abilities, spiritual gifts, and material resources within the church. Liberal financial giving is one vital way for the steward to support the church's worship, fellowship, education, service, and proclamation to the ends of the earth.

A responsible steward will not leave his gift at the altar and then ignore what it is used for. The giving steward should also participate in the decision-making processes of the congregation to ensure that his gifts are used efficiently, targeted toward purposes that are central to the kingdom of God, and equitably distributed so that they support the many dimensions of the church's worldwide ministry. Through giving and participating, the steward can help the church to be the church.

Major Concerns in Giving to the Church

Why should the steward give to the church and not just indiscriminately to worthy needs and causes in general? The imperative to give to the church presumes that the church channels money to particular causes related to the central concerns of the kingdom of God. How should the church expend money given by its members? There is no detailed set of instructions on that. But the New Testament's description of central concerns within the apostolic church can provide

99

illuminating clues as to what is perennially important for the church's use of finances.

There were four prominent financial concerns in the apostolic church. Three of those were shared in the Old Testament tradition of giving. (1) A first concern was the support of ministers. The principle is that a worker is worthy of his hire; so those who preach the gospel should be supported by the gospel (see Matt. 10:10; I Cor. 9:14). (2) The apostolic church also utilized funds to care for the needs of church members, particularly their own widows, orphans, and poor (see I Tim. 5:17). (3) The concern for needy fellow Christians extended to those in other congregations, as in the Jerusalem relief offering (see II Cor. 8, 9). (4) Gifts to the church also supported the church's mission to the world, a cause not paralleled in the Old Testament. Traveling missionaries, evangelists, and others were financed by the church (see I Cor. 9:11; II Cor. 12:13).

How should the church translate those concerns into channels of giving for today? Given the variety of church life and the differing conceptions of priorities within the kingdom of God, that decision can be made only by particular congregations and denominations. The church must always support the professional ministry, care for human needs, and fund its mission in the world. But the particulars are not always so clear. There are critical internal and external dimensions of the church's life. The inner needs include worship, education, the nurture of spiritual disciplines, the enrichment of community life, and other specialized concerns. The inner need generally involves buildings and other facilities. The church still ought to provide for the needs of its members, a ministry increasingly more formalized in caring institutions. Giving still supports the external ministry and mission of the church, ranging from its immediate locale around the world. Giving to the church enables each Christian to participate in the whole mission of the church, to go where he cannot personally go, to serve people he will never meet.

The Steward's Gift to the Church

Proportionate giving is the key to the Christian's giving to the church. But what portion of his income should that be? Since the beginning of modern stewardship efforts, many Christians have assumed that the tithe is the standard of Christian giving. Aware of the dangers of legalism, many churches have developed a rationale for the tithe that gains the benefits of a precise standard without succumbing to the dangers of an indiscriminate Old Testament legalism. The logic usually is that the Hebrews gave a tithe to the temple; so the Christian who is under grace would surely not do less. So the tithe is the minimum starting point for Christian giving. With that line of logic, the tithe is then advocated as the New Testament standard of giving.

That appears to be a tidy piece of logic. The problem is that the New Testament nowhere contains a specific commandment that the Christian should tithe. The tithe is mentioned only three times in the New Testament—in Matthew 23:23 (with a parallel in Luke 11:42), Luke 18:12, and Hebrews 7:1-10; and in each case the allusion to the tithe is merely incidental to another point being made. Beyond these references there is no other mention of the tithe in the whole New Testament. If that were the clear standard of giving in the New Testament church, it would have been useful to appeal to the tithe in the major giving passages in the New Testament. But in those passages—like II Corinthians 8 and 9, I Timothy 6, and I Corinthians 16:1-4—there is not the slightest hint of the tithe.

Many people honestly assume that the tithe is taught in the New Testament and then proceed to quote Old Testament tithing passages. But even the Old Testament picture is not quite so simple. Unquestionably, the practice of the tithe has ancient roots in many cultures. The tithe had several purposes in Israel's religious practice. The tithes of all agricultural products honored God as owner of the land and giver of the produce, supported the temple and priesthood, and provided for many charitable needs.

Old Testament tithing traditions are complex and difficult to unravel with certainty. Most scholars hold that there were three diverse tithing traditions in the Old Testament that were later harmonized in Judaism. The rabbis prescribed three annual tithes based upon Numbers 18:21-24, Deuteronomy 12:5-19 and 14:22-23, and Deuteronomy 12:28-29. Depending upon how the tithes were calculated, they totaled either 20 percent or 23½ percent of the giver's total income. These were basically agricultural tithes, and F. C. Grant contends that there was no tithe imposed upon artisans, tradesmen, fishermen, and others, including diaspora Jews.[9]

F. C. Grant, one of the major authorities on the subject, has shown that in the time of Jesus, Judaism had twelve regularly prescribed tithes and offerings and, in addition, the requirement to give alms to the needy.[10] The combined religious tithes and offerings plus the Roman tax totaled in the range of 40 percent of the strict tither's income. It is simply not historically accurate to assume that the devout Jew gave precisely 10 percent, that Jesus as a devout Jew gave 10 percent, and therefore the Christian should give 10 percent. That is questionable logic based upon debatable assumptions.

What, then, should be the amount of the Christian's giving? The New Testament is not specific on that question. Jesus praised the widow who gave her mite, because it was everything she had (see Mark 12:40). Zaccheus repaid four times more those whom he had cheated and gave one-half of his goods to the poor (see Matt. 19:21; Luke 12:33). Jesus commanded the rich young ruler to sell all that he had and give it to the poor (see Matt. 19:21). In the unusual situation of the early Jerusalem church, many of the Christians had all things in common. Some sold property to share the money with others (see Acts 2:44-45; 4:37; 5:1-11).

What is clear is that early Christians practiced generous sacrificial giving. However, since the New Testament does not advocate a technical percentage, we too should be hesitant to insist on any legalistic and technical approach to giving. But the biblical principles will lead to openhanded liberal giving. It is possible through these principles to undergird financially the work of the church, help the individual fulfill his stewardship obligations, and at the same preserve his responsible freedom and facilitate his growth as a person.

Proportionate giving is the standard. Whatever else the principle of the tithe says to the church, it does indicate that each Christian should give as God has blessed him with material goods. In any age, a sizable amount of the Christian's income should be given to the work of the church. The Macedonian contribution to the Jerusalem church remains an example of generous proportionate giving. Paul comments that they "gave according to their means . . . and beyond their means, . . . begging us earnestly for the favor of taking part in the relief of the saints" (II Cor. 8:3-4). That is liberal, generous, sacrificial giving.

Ordinary Christians often want guidance in determining how much of their income to give in the service of the Kingdom. And here the concept of the tithe can be a valuable model for Christian giving. The tithe is a principle hallowed in historical usage, one that runs through the Old Testament back into many ancient societies. If taken as a starting point from which individual Christians begin to determine what portion of their income represents sacrificial stewardship in giving, then the tithe is a useful model. In general it is the case that most Christians under grace will not be less sacrificial in giving than were tithers under the Old Testament law. *Most Christians perhaps should ideally give at least a tithe of their income.*

The problem arises when that principle is turned into a legalistic demand. Then the tithe can be too little for some people and might impose excessive difficulty upon others. By far the majority of contemporary Christians can give a tithe without any real sacrifice. However, there are people today for whom the tithe would be an exorbitant demand, if made by the church. For example, there are many elderly people living strictly on limited Social Security income in a skyrocketing inflationary economy and people who incur devasting medical bills in critical long-term illnesses. They must be free to determine what proportion of their income can represent sacrificial love for God. And some will *choose* to tithe! On the other hand, for some affluent Christians the tithe would represent very limited love when compared to the income used for other purposes. Many of the affluent should be encouraged to give generously beyond the tithe. There is a difference when the tithe is used as a model and not as a universal rule.

Congregations and the Church

Where should one give within the life of the church? Various modern churches and denominations hold different views about the relationships within the church, ranging from the individual congregation to the larger horizons of the life of the church, including the denomination and other ecumenical relationships. The congregation or parish is the usual focal point of the Christian's giving. But many of the church's mission commitments in the world are supported cooperatively by the wider structures of the church.

The Christian's gifts support a wide variety of modern ministries. In many denominations these include home and foreign mission work, educational institutions, hospitals, children's homes, retirement homes, social ministries, Christian camps, and other specialized concerns. Methods of financial support of these types of ministries vary among denominations. In numerous cases, they receive denominational or national church allocations as well as support by individual Christians. Some modern Christians also choose to give to independent or parachurch groups and to causes outside the normal channels of their own church's life.

How should the individual determine whether and when to give to various Christian causes? As a general principle, one's first line of obligation is to the congregation and through its ties to the larger church and covenant commitments of that particular family of faith. That responsibility is assumed when one joins a particular congregation and denominational group. One's giving to the church ought to start with the congregation within which the individual lives, participates, and benefits.

Many Christians have specialized concerns and commitments throughout the spectrum of the church's ministries and mission. At times some Christians want to concentrate their giving in specific areas. This is particularly true of Christians with accumulated wealth. Numerous church institutions depend upon generous above-and-beyond giving. Such direct giving can benefit both institutions and individuals. Direct financial gifts help institutions stabilize their long-range plans. Because direct giving to these causes involves the giver and his gift with the beneficiary of his gift, it often provides a joy that is not so possible in less direct forms of giving. What is critical for responsible stewardship is that institutional giving not become a substitute for responsible giving to one's church congregation and the *total* balanced commitment of his own covenant community.

The question of designated giving. Should the giver ever designate his gifts to the church? As a general principle, the giver should avoid designated giving. The reason? As a member of a covenant community, he should accept the will of the congregation about its life and work, including its judgment about financial priorities and expenditures, unless he must do otherwise as a matter of conscience or as a particular extraordinary commitment.

There could be exceptions to this general principle. At times a large undesignated gift to the general budget could be counterproductive and prompt others in the church to diminish their own level of giving. Or there could be times when the church itself is an irresponsible steward of the funds entrusted to it. The church might become overcommitted to impressive buildings and ignore human concerns. Or the church might neglect some critical dimension of the biblical imperatives for ministry and mission. Or the church might appropriate large funds for highly questionable purposes.

When there is a breakdown of collective stewardship, the steward might ideally attempt to lead the congregation to recapture proper priorities. In cases where that effort fails, the steward's individual responsibility becomes the dominating factor. He may then choose reluctantly to designate his gifts. One caution should be noted. The Christian should never use designated giving capriciously or maliciously as a political weapon within the church. That is an abuse of responsible freedom.

The special problems of the wealthy. People of substantial wealth or other people who accumulate large sums of money over the years face special problems in deciding how to give large amounts of money. This could involve large weekly proportionate gifts from high income or large special gifts from accumulated wealth. If a wealthy individual should tithe an amount equal to the whole budget of his congregation, then his gift might have an unfortunate impact. Other church members could then minimize their own financial responsibility to the church. Or the wealthy person could seek a position of political power equal to the size of his gifts.

One solution is for the wealthy person to give a modest undesignated offering to the general budget of a church and to designate the remainder to other causes in the larger ministry of the church. Large individual gifts like bequests, endowments, and memorials pose similar problems. A responsible approach for the wealthy could be to give large gifts to the congregation for its capital needs, but not for regular operating funds or for endowment that would provide future operating funds. These should be given by the whole church. But there are no hard and fast rules. Here, as elsewhere, there is no substitute for the responsible freedom of the individual steward.

Giving Outside the Church

Christian giving encompasses more than giving to the church and church-related concerns. One of the purposes of giving is to meet the needs of the human family. Legitimate needs emerge at various levels, beginning with one's own family, local community, nation, and the worldwide human family. Our modern problem is how to discriminate among the numerous voices clamoring for financial support. The principle of responsible freedom is the only sufficient basis upon which the church can help Christians decide when, where, and how much to give to causes outside the immediate life of the church.

Giving to One's Family Needs

The care of one's own family needs is a high priority in Christian giving. Biblical thought regards this as a religious duty of first importance. Paul's warning ought to inform the teaching of the church and the practice of individuals: "If any one does not provide for . . . his own family, he has disowned the faith and is worse than an unbeliever" (I Tim. 5:8). At a minimum that principle should apply to one's care of children, a spouse, and parents.

There are specialized problems in today's society that could have severe budgetary impact on Christian families, even to the point of affecting what they can give to the church. For example, there is the care of elderly parents. Fortunately, many developed countries have substantial social programs that provide for older people. But none of these programs can relieve the Christian of the obligation to assure that the basic needs of his elderly parents are met. Another unusual problem relates to the current disintegration of the American family. The high divorce rate creates new dimensions of the need to care for one's own family. In many cases, divorced persons are forced to maintain two households and to live within severe budgetary constraints. Other examples are the escalating costs of medical care and

107

education, which often force American families into substantial indebtedness.

How should the church relate the care of family to other aspects of Christian giving? There is no simple answer. But the church should be understanding about the exceptional family situations in which extraordinary costs for unusual family care may force church members against their own desires to cut back on the amount they give to the church. There are instances when gifts less than a tithe might represent sacrificial giving at that juncture of their lives. The stewardship of giving ought to be interpreted in a way that allows them to experience the joy of giving, even when the amount is not what they would genuinely like to give and ideally should give.

What is not acceptable is for the church to take a legalistic approach that demands that a person must tithe at a minimum to be in good standing or to serve in a place of leadership, whatever his family obligations. The church should be guided here by Jesus' condemnation of Jews who avoided their responsibility to needy parents by the device of declaring their wealth "Corban," meaning it was reserved for God (see Mark 7:11). If the individual has no right to avoid parental responsibilities for "temple reasons," then the church has no right to declare the individual's wealth corban if it means he must neglect an even more fundamental obligation—the care of parents and family.

Direct Giving to Immediate Human Need

The Bible repeatedly underlines the Christian's responsibility to people in need. Jesus regarded almsgiving as a chief duty of man (see Matt. 6:2-4). Jesus praised the good Samaritan's spontaneous gift to the injured traveler (see Luke 10:29-37). Zaccheus gave one-half of his wealth to the poor (see Luke 19:8). Jesus teaches that persons who give to the poor will be rewarded at the resurrection (see Luke 14:14). He even indicates that giving to the hungry, thirsty, stranger, naked, and imprisoned is giving to the Lord himself (see

Matt. 25:31-46). In the parable of the good Samaritan, Jesus warns about the danger of being so caught up in "churchly" concerns that we become indifferent to human need as we meet it face-to-face.

The Christian should exercise love and intelligent discrimination in giving directly to human need. Giving and loving are not necessarily the same thing. Paul warns, "If I give away all I have, . . . but have not love, I gain nothing"(I Cor. 13:3). Loveless giving can represent nothing more than conscience money for long-neglected social inequities within our communities. Giving should be discriminating, designed not merely to meet immediate need but to help people toward self-sufficiency. In this way, the Christian steward can make investments that produce rich dividends in personhood and human development.

Giving to Organized Secular Charities

Caring is not confined to the church. Many sensitive human services operate outside the life of the church. Diverse organized charities are an important ingredient of modern society. Numerous charitable organizations offer valuable and essential human services that were once provided by the church. Most communities now coordinate contributions to many of these charities through the United Fund or Community Chest. As a responsible citizen, the Christian will normally want to contribute to many of these causes. Because of giving generous portions of his income to the church, the Christian can often be somewhat more limited than nonchurch citizens in the amount he can give to these causes. But if the Christian neglects them, he then forces non-Christians to bear complete responsibility.

For that reason, the church ought to encourage participation in community charitable causes. In cases where individuals cannot conscientiously support all United Fund causes, it is possible to designate gifts for specific organizations. The Christian should have a wholistic human approach to life.

Giving to Nonchurch Institutions and Causes

God's purpose in creation and redemption concerns the whole of life and the world. Because all things have been reconciled to God in Christ, the Christian faith rejects our modern division of life into secular and sacred spheres. Whatever contributes to personal life is blessed by God unless it is perverted. The Christian is a citizen of two worlds—of this world and of the world to come. As a citizen of this world, the Christian is responsible for a wide range of human endeavors—education, science, the arts, natural resources, and various cultural and aesthetic values. Many worthy, contemporary human causes require private financial support. The Christian can legitimately contribute to any cause that enhances the beauty, enjoyment, understanding, and humanness of life.

There are vast global economic and social needs to which Christians can contribute. Various organizations work in the less-developed countries of the world and in areas of military conflict. Christians might want to give aid to war or disaster victims, refugees, undernourished children, the poor, or people needing medical care. Dozens of programs deserve support.

There are also noble national projects, ranging from social needs to the areas of culture, the arts, education, scientific research, or ecology. The problem is how to determine what causes should claim priority. A guiding principle for the Christian might be to give first to causes that alleviate human misery or enrich life or advance the frontiers of the human spirit. All these human concerns honor God too!

VIII
The Stewardship
of the Church

The church is a stewardship community that is central in the purposes of God for human history. Many references of specific stewardship words in the New Testament are to various aspects of the church's life and ministry. If God's purposes in creation and redemption might be described as the divine art of person-making, then the church is essential to God's whole creative-redemptive process. We become persons and fully human within community. The church represents the beginning of that new humanity that God is calling into being.

The Ephesians writer in particular eloquently describes the crucial role of the church's stewardship within the divine purposes. After depicting God's act of redemption in Christ and Christ's present lordship in human history, he states that God "has put all things under his feet and has made him the head over all things *for the church,* which is his body" (Eph. 1:22-23; see 1:3-10; emphasis added). The church is a key participant in God's plan (*oikonomia* = stewardship) for the ages, "that through the church the manifold wisdom of God might now be made known" (Eph. 3:10). Redemption is into the church. All people—Jew and Gentile—are reconciled to God in one body through the cross (see Eph. 2:16). Ephesians specifically ties life in the church to a stewardship participation in God's plan (*oikonomia*) when it states that Christians are "fellow citizens with the saints and members of the household of God [*oikos tou theou*]" (Eph. 2:19-22). Other stewardship references detail the role of individual believers within the church.

The image of the church as "the household of God" provides a constructive starting point for understanding the church's stewardship of all its resources—human, spiritual, and material—in the service of God (see Eph. 2:19-22; I Tim. 3:15). The Greek words for the household of God (*oikos tou theou*) specifically relate the church to a whole constellation of stewardship vocabulary and ideas using the root word "house" (*oikos*). To be God's steward (*oikonomos*) and to exercise responsible stewardship (*oikonomia*) involves one in the household of God (*oikos tou theou*) where the Christian is edified (*oikodome*). Everything within the church's stewardship of its resources should contribute to the edification and uniting of the church in Christ as a preparation for its ministry and mission in the world (see Eph. 4:29; I Cor. 14:12).

According to the New Testament, every Christian shares in the stewardship of the household of God. The New Testament uses the term *steward* for every member of the church, from the apostles throughout the ranks of believers (see I Cor. 4:1 f.; Titus 1:7; I Pet. 4:10). Spheres of responsibility extend from the congregation to the universal church. The resources for which the church is collectively responsible include the gospel itself, leadership, human beings, material wealth, and anything else that enables the church to be the church and do its work in the world.

The church is accountable before God for its faithfulness to its own calling and for how it uses its resources in the service of God's purposes in creation and redemption. The criterion of accountability will be how well the church actualizes in practice its theology of the nature, ministry, and mission of the church. The stewardship model thus offers a way for the church to integrate its varied concerns and responsibilities into an overarching concept of stewardship management.

The Nature, Ministry, and Mission of the Church

In a brief chapter, we cannot develop an exhaustive theology of the church. Our concern is not to state or evaluate the classic doctrines of the church but to highlight aspects of a theology of the church that illuminate its stewardship role. The doctrine of the church is a divisive issue in the contemporary church. Although ecclesiologies may differ, most Christian communions would agree that the church is the people of God, composed of persons who have been reconciled to God through faith in Jesus Christ, and who are bound to Christ, their head, and to one another through the Holy Spirit. As the elect people of God, the church is called out (*ekklesia*) of the world into the new creation in Christ and sent out (*apostello*) into the world in the power of the Spirit to serve in Christ's name and to make known the good news of the gospel.

Any full-scale theology of the church must stress the multidimensionality of the church's nature and mission—its continuity as a "called out" community with the ancient people of God (I Pet. 2:9), its embodiment of the new humanity and new age which broke into history in Jesus Christ, and its life, ministry, and mission in the power of the Spirit. Out of its many images and theological insights, the New Testament teaches that the purposes of God in creation and redemption are substantially actualized within and through the church.

Of all the images and descriptions of the church, the symbol of reconciliation perhaps most incisively portrays the personal and relational dimensions of the church's life and stewardship. Without ignoring or oversimplifying the importance of a full-scale theology of the church, one might simply describe the church as a community of reconciliation where people have been reconciled to God through faith in Christ and are in the process of being reconciled to themselves and to other persons. The reconciled community has committed to it a ministry and message of reconciliation (see II Cor. 5:18-20). The church is called to develop that new style of reconciled life within, and then to let it flow out into the world.

Internally, the church is a community of reconciliation. It is involved in developing persons, in the full meaning of personhood within community, in accordance with God's personal purposes in the created order. There in the fellowship of the Spirit and through mutual love and care (see I Cor. 12:25), human beings are in the process of becoming persons who have attained "to mature manhood, to the measure of the stature of the fulness of Christ" (Eph. 4:13). Every ministry of the church must be measured by God's purposes in the reconciliation of persons.

Ministry represents how the church does its mission, both in terms of internal community and of external penetration of the world. The style of that ministry is servanthood, in which Christians are servants to one another and to the whole world (see Mark 10:43-45). Ministry properly takes place in the inner and the outer life of the church, one to *effect* reconciliation in community, the other to *call* to reconciliation in community. There is a mutual ministry within the church that facilitates the growth of people toward personal and spiritual maturity and that enables their ministry in the world. The reconciling commitment of the church should determine the focus, approach, and structure of the church's internal life, as ways of helping the whole community of faith toward human-spiritual maturity.

The church, however, is not an end in itself. It is also God's instrument in the world. Mission represents God's sending out the church in a ministry of reconciliation through which mankind is redeemed into a new life of reconciled humanity. The church is a missionary people, commissioned by Christ and empowered by the Spirit for that task. There should be no confusion about the gospel's being at the heart of that mission. The servant of Christ is also a bearer of the good news. As Ferdinand Hahn has observed, "For the whole New Testament there is no missionary preaching and activity that does not involve making known the Christ-event to the whole world and proclaiming to all mankind the salvation that has become manifest in Christ."[11]

The Church's Stewardship Resources

The stewardship of the church will be measured by its faithfulness in using its resources—spiritual, human, and material—to fulfill its own nature, ministry, and mission. The individual congregation is a primary area of the church's stewardship responsibility. Within the congregation the family relationship is most intimately experienced, spiritual edification occurs, and ministry is extended. Many of those responsibilities also extend into the larger structures of the church beyond the congregation. The New Testament specifically calls for the stewardship of certain important resources within the church.

The Stewardship of the Gospel

The church is steward of the gospel. The New Testament describes the church, particularly as centered in the apostles, as steward of the mysteries of God that are now revealed to it (see I Cor. 4:1 ff.; I Thess. 2:1-20). Those mysteries concern God's own stewardship plan (*oikonomia*) of salvation for the fullness of time, his purpose and claim upon the universe through his reconciliation of the world to himself in Christ (see Eph. 1:10). That secret is now proclaimed by the church (see Col. 1:25-26).

The church is commissioned to preserve the gospel's integrity (see I Tim. 6:20; et al.). That responsibility rests heavily upon leaders of the church such as pastors and teachers. Paul admonishes the bishop or pastor to be a careful workman, "rightly handling the word of truth" (II Tim. 2:15) and confuting those who contradict it (see Titus 1:9). The implications are substantial for the church's theological reflection, preaching, and teaching.

The church, further, has an education-evangelism function to share the gospel with every person in the world. The Ephesians writer speaks of himself, but his words apply to all Christians when he says, "This grace was given, to preach to the Gentiles the unsearchable riches of Christ, and to make all men see what is the plan [*oikonomia*] of the mystery hidden for

115

ages in God who created all things" (Eph. 3:8-10). The church is commissioned to help direct the thrust of life in accordance with God's will as revealed in Christ.

The Stewardship of Church Leaders

Every Christian is a steward within the church. Yet there are functional dimensions of stewardship that fall upon leaders of the church. The New Testament's guidance on the stewardship of the apostles and bishops would apply to a whole range of professional church leadership. The term *steward* is used specifically for apostles and bishops. Although there is not an exact parallel to the apostle today, the apostolic stewardship continues to have relevance to the contemporary church. It underlines the importance of faithfully maintaining the nature and pattern of the apostolic church and the apostolic witness to Christ (see I Cor. 3:10-15; 4:1-5).

At a more direct level, the New Testament also applies the term *steward* to leaders of individual congregations. Paul says, for example, that "a bishop, as God's steward, must be blameless" (Titus 1:7). He then catalogs the bishop's special stewardship requirements. The requirements touch upon his personhood, self-control, character and behavior, social relationships, values, commitment to the integrity of the gospel, and skills in interpreting it. The contemporary leader too must be faithful to his understanding of his calling and office, to the particular job responsibilities he accepts, and to the functions he must perform. He must be a good steward of his specific gifts for and tasks in ministry.

The professional leader also carries a stewardship responsibility as an enabler within the congregation. Ephesians 4:11 describes that task as one of equipping the saints for the work of the ministry. A leader is to inspire, challenge, and lift the horizons of his fellow believers. He is to interpret the gospel so as to facilitate the growth of persons in their stewardship of life and participation in the stewardship of the church and society. A major test of a pastor's or other leader's stewardship will be the degree to which he enables other lay Christians to do their ministries.

The Stewardship of Persons

Human beings are the most valuable resource within the church. Creation and redemption are God's way of developing authentic mature persons. Therefore, the church's stewardship will be largely measured by what happens to people in the flow of its life. At the heart of the church's programming and style of community must be the affirmation of the essential worth and importance of every person in the life and ministry of the church. The major internal ministries should be designed to contribute to that personal development and to respect the integrity of personhood. The church must avoid any program or process that manipulates persons or relieves them of responsibility for their own lives.

Among the many images of the church, the image of the church as the Body of Christ is a fertile picture of the place and dignity of each person within the Christian community. The Body of Christ is an organic model of the church, one in which each member is essential to the healthy functioning of the organism which is more than the sum of its parts. Individualism and corporate relationships are reconciled in Christ who is the head of the Body. Individuals most fully realize themselves when they are most open to others in the church. And the community is healthiest when it most respects the integrity and importance of its individual members (see I Cor. 12, 13; Rom. 12).

The stewardship of human resources also requires the church to help people to discover and develop their particular gifts for ministry. It is basic to the New Testament to affirm that each believer has a ministry to perform within the Body of Christ and that the Spirit gives each member a spiritual gift for that purpose. The source of each person's gift is God's grace (see Rom. 12:6). Because of the multiple needs, there are varieties of gifts, service, and workings within the church that are distributed individually by the Holy Spirit as he wills

117

(see I Cor. 12:4-6). Their purpose is to serve the common good of the Body of Christ (see I Cor. 12:7). Each person is to discover his gift, develop it, and put it to work in the church's ministry. The church should establish procedures that uncover and utilize those gifts within its membership. First Peter 4:10 specifically connects the use of spiritual gifts with one's stewardship: "As each has received a gift [charisma], employ it for one another, as good stewards [oikonomoi] of God's varied grace." The stewardship goal for every congregation ought to be: every Christian a minister!

The Stewardship of Financial Resources

Just as the individual's stewardship of material resources reflects his values and ordering of life, so does the church's use of its material resources reflect its priorities and spiritual health. Corporate financial stewardship refers primarily to how the church acquires and uses its finances. The church, from the congregation through wider ecclesiastical structures, should encourage responsible financial stewardship for each member and practice good stewardship at every level of its own corporate life.

The church has an interpreting and facilitating role for its members that goes beyond its concerns with giving to the church. It should inspire and assist its members in the total stewardship of their material resources. That would include sensitizing them (1) to Christian values about material things and attitudes toward the world; (2) to the stewardship of all one's material wealth, not just giving; (3) to the practice of individual or family budgeting and financial planning; and (4) to a caring, sharing, sacrificial life-style. In terms of giving, the church should encourage (1) the stewardship of total giving, including such specialized matters as large gifts and the final disposition of estates, and (2) the practice of generous proportionate giving of one's income to the church and the work of the Kingdom.

The theological idea of the priesthood of believers has important implications for the church's financial steward-

118

ship. As a way of expressing the universal ministry of the church, it means that each believer shares in doing the work of the church and therefore of discerning God's will for the church, including the use of financial resources. Each church member should participate in giving, budgeting, and expending of church finances. The church thus integrates personal and corporate responsibilities. The good steward cannot merely give and then abandon responsibility for the use of the gift to a small group within the congregation or denomination.

The church should develop a comprehensive financial stewardship program. Its purpose must be far more than that of raising money for operating needs, capital projects, or special concerns or ministries. It should encompass the multiple dimensions of stewardship. A major aspect ought to be related to the support of vital Christian ministries through systematic, proportionate giving. That involves both the stewardship of giving and of the use of funds in Christian ministries. Giving and spending are inseparable.

The stewardship of giving. The church fills a vital role in the stewardship of giving. The church cannot be a good steward of its material resources without urging generous, joyful, sacrificial giving to the church. And because of the importance of giving, the church should not be hesitant, embarrassed, or apologetic in doing so. The following principles may be useful suggestions for helping the church toward a person-centered, mission-oriented program of giving.

1. Make giving an essential part of the worship experience.

2. Teach biblical principles of financial stewardship as an integral part of the Christian stewardship of life, and do it on a regular basis.

3. Relate Christian giving to the support of vital ministries, and clearly and regularly interpret these to the congregation.

4. Encourage giving to a unified general budget in which

119

the whole church participates in determining priorities and allocating funds.

5. Utilize a pledge or subscription program in connection with the yearly budget. Design it as a nonmanipulative interpretation of the biblical principles of motivation and method in giving.

6. Minimize special appeals, except when necessary in emergencies or when integrated into the church's total budget.

7. Reject money-raising projects that appeal to sub-Christian standards and that become a substitute for individual sacrificial giving.

8. Reject any program that manipulates people or appeals to unacceptable motivational principles.

9. Establish a church policy on endowment funds and memorial gifts that does not relieve the congregation of its continuing weekly responsibility to give in support of the church's ministries and that equally respects the good stewardship of all church members.

The stewardship of spending. The stewardship of spending offers a way for the church to find and do the will of God. The unified budget is the *best* method by which the whole church can share in the corporate responsibility of financial stewardship. A budget makes good business sense for the orderly receiving and expending of finances. The budget-planning process and an accompanying budget subscription program can give a yearly opportunity for the church to reexamine its life and work and to elicit new commitments of persons as well as financial pledges. The stewardship campaign should be a major educational effort about the nature and ministry of the church.

Churches looking for better stewardship ideas might consider *mission-action budgeting* as a way of experiencing a yearly reevaluation of spending and a renewal of the church's commitment to mission. The following suggestions can help do that.

1. Justify all budgetary allocations on the basis of priorities

that grow out of the church's definition of its own nature and mission.

2. Involve the whole church in the budget-making process, and program the whole process to involve a reassessment of what the church is and of the mission it should attempt.

3. Ask hard questions! Is this item, program, building, or other expenditure basic to what the church is about?

4. Adopt the budget in a Sunday morning worship service so that it is not merely a business decision but an expression of spiritual vision and personal and corporate commitment.

5. Follow up the adoption of the budget with a nonmanipulative subscription effort that seeks to involve every church member in the church's financial stewardship.

Perhaps not all churches will order their budgetary priorities in quite the same way. However, there are important legitimate concerns that ought to have substantial allocations within a church's budget. These are:

1. *World mission.* The church should allocate a generous portion of its budget to the world horizons of ministry and mission through its appropriate denominational or ecumenical agencies. The principle of proportionate giving should apply to churches as well as to individuals, specifically to their involvement in ministries outside their own congregation's local ministries. A caring, mission-oriented church will provide substantial support for community, home, and foreign missions, Christian education, theological education, human causes of many kinds, mass communication of the gospel, and many other ministries essential to the worldwide impact of the gospel. The church cannot exercise good stewardship if it turns in upon itself and forgets the world it is called to serve.

2. *Local ministries.* Internal ministries of the church require substantial expenditures. Those should be funded within the congregation's own understanding of the nature and mission of the church. These would normally include worship, music, education, leadership training, fellowship, recrea-

tion, evangelism, and social ministries to a variety of special people. These might be children, the elderly, handicapped people, disadvantaged people, and perhaps others, depending upon a church's location and vision.

The church can utilize the budget-making process for a continuing assessment of its old ministries and inquiry into potential new ministries. Churches can get locked into a budgeting pattern that reflects institutional and program paralysis and rigidity. Organizations and programs originally designed for mission can over a period of years become self-perpetuating ends in themselves long after outliving their usefulness. The budget process can help churches bury dead programs and birth new mission ministries.

3. *Financial provision for professional ministers.* This should be a top priority. Many churches are guilty of poor stewardship in the low salaries they pay their professional staff ministers and denominational servants. Adequate salaries for professional personnel make good business sense as well as good stewardship. No one can work at maximum effectiveness when saddled with anxiety about paying bills at a survival level. Professional ministers are not called to any greater financial sacrifice than are other members of the church. At the same time, generous support has reasonable limits. As Peter warns, elders are not to tend the flock for shameful gain (see I Pet. 5:2).

4. *Building and property.* The typical modern church would find it difficult to function without the buildings in which its varied activities take place. However, many sensitive Christians now question the disproportionate amount of money invested in church property and facilities. Excessive building debts frequently require money that is needed for vital ministries. Given the current high cost of land and construction, churches need to ask honest questions about whether a proposed building project is necessary and about how it will help the church to implement its purpose. The church ought to probe its own motives. In some instances, the buildings represent frills or satisfaction of ego needs. But

when the church determines that the buildings are vital to its basic purpose, then the church should build functional and aesthetically satisfying buildings that do not flout ostentatious luxury. New buildings or minimally used old buildings may offer the church an unexpected opportunity to devise new ministries that justify their cost.

Denominational and Ecumenical Stewardship

The church's stewardship extends beyond the congregation to denominations and ecumenical structures, formal or informal, that are also expressions of the church's nature and mission. Given the diversity of contemporary fragmented Christianity, one cannot easily generalize about denominational stewardship. Yet it is vital from several standpoints. One critical value is that Christian stewardship ought rightly to express the essential unity of the one church of Jesus Christ on earth. In the words of Ephesians, "There is one body and one Spirit, . . . one hope . . . , one Lord, one faith, one baptism, one God and Father of us all, who is above all and through all and in all" (Eph. 4:4-6). Theologically and practically, the whole Body of Christ on earth must together attempt to accomplish God's work in the world.

Beyond the theological basis of the whole church's ministry, contemporary denominational and ecumenical structures and arrangements have utilitarian value in providing a way for the concentrated commitments and energy of individual congregations to engage in mission and ministry that cannot be achieved at the local level. Out of these structures flow different contemporary ministries such as hospitals, educational institutions, homes for the aged or for children, Christian social centers, and the wide range of home and foreign missions.

American denominations have varied polities from congregational to episcopal, and different denominational structures within those polities. So one cannot define how stewardship should work in particular communions. However, several general principles can have application in any

Christian communion. Denominational stewardship should embody the following principles.

1. All programs and ministries should be designed to implement in practice the nature and mission of the church.

2. Denominational stewardship should respect the value and integrity of persons who are servants of their constituencies, so that personnel policies and relationships do not merely imitate those of secular corporations.

3. All denominational agencies and personnel should efficiently use their abilities and spiritual gifts in the service of the church and efficiently use the church's money in order to minimize administrative costs and to maximize its contribution to human need and vital church ministries.

4. Denominational bodies and agencies should continually reassess expenditures and ministries in light of changing circumstance and need.

5. Denominational and ecumenical bodies should be sensitive to the will of their constituencies in determining how money will be used, particularly regarding controversial and tangential programs that can be debated by sensitive, perceptive Christians. The church's leadership must learn to walk the difficult line between the abandonment of prophetic risk and the disregard of the collective judgment of their constituencies.

There are inherent dangers within any large organizational structure. For one thing, power intoxicates and corrupts. That can be unusually devastating when subtly cloaked in the piety of ecclesiastical circles. In addition, bureaucracy tends to be self-perpetuating, so that it almost inevitably entrenches, expands, and works to justify its own existence. Organizational structures also easily become rigid, and people working within them come to regard them as ends and not means, and then abandon prophetic self-criticism. In a consummate way, a word of Jesus applies to servants in church structures at any level: "Every one to whom much is given, of him will much be required; and of him to whom men commit much they will demand the more" (Luke 12:47).

With this brief final look at the church's corporate stewardship, we have now seen how Christian stewardship can serve as a model for creative living. It integrates many dimensions of the individual's life and participation in the church and the world into the understanding of God as owner, man as steward, and the world as the stage for the drama of creation and redemption. At every level, God's personal purposes are pivotal, and man's life before God in freedom and responsibility are critical elements in his growth into full personhood in relation to God and man. Ultimately, man is accountable before God for management of all the resources entrusted to man as an individual and as part of the human family. If the steward lives his stewardship well, there is hope that at the time of final accountability, he will hear from the divine Master, "Well done, good and faithful servant; you have been faithful over a little, I will set you over much; enter into the joy of your master" (Matt. 25:23).

Notes

1. Otto Michel, *"Oikos—oikoumene," Theological Dictionary of the New Testament,* ed. Gerhard Kittel and Gerhard Friedrich, trans. Geoffrey W. Bromiley (Grand Rapids: Eerdmans Publishing Co., 1967), vol. 5: 119-59.
2. The words are used more frequently for such things as God's plan of salvation (see Eph. 1:10; 3:9), the apostolic office (see I Cor. 9:17; Col. 1:25; et al.), other office-bearers in the church (see Titus 1:7), and for all Christians and the stewardship of their spiritual gifts (see I Pet. 4:10-11).
3. For excellent theological studies of stewardship, see Helge Brattgard, *God's Stewards,* trans. Gene J. Lund (Minneapolis: Augsburg Publishing House, 1963), and T. A. Kantonen, *A Theology for Christian Stewardship* (Philadelphia: Muhlenberg Press, 1956).
4. Michel, *"Oikos—oikoumene,"* p. 152. In the Pauline epistles, *oikonomia* can refer to the apostolic office or to the divine plan of salvation, and it is not always clear which is intended.
5. *Miracles: A Preliminary Study* (New York: The Macmillan Co., 1947), p. 107.
6. For a brief discussion of the terms, see C. R. North, "The World," *The Interpreter's Dictionary of the Bible* (Nashville: Abingdon Press, 1962), vol. 4: 873-78.
7. *Man in the Old Testament* (London: SCM Press, 1951), p. 33.
8. Dietrich Bonhoeffer, *Ethics,* trans N. H. Smith (New York: The Macmillan Co., 1955), pp. 125 ff.

9. *The Economic Background of the Gospels* (New York: Oxford University Press, 1926), pp. 92-100.
10. Ibid.
11. *Mission in the New Testament*, trans. Frank Clarke (Naperville, Ill.: Alec R. Allenson, 1965), p. 169.